When the Heart Won't Let Go

Breaking Negative Patterns Series

Book II

*The Step-by-Step Manual to
Releasing the Heart from Stress
and Moving Beyond Grief,
Hurt, and Anxiety*

Books in the Breaking Negative Patterns Series

Breaking Negative Patterns
Includes the strongholds of Bitterness, Confusion, Control, Deception, Depression, Discouragement, Dysfunction, Fatigue, and Injustice.

Breaking Negative Patterns
Workbook

Breaking Negative Patterns
Spanish Edition

When the Heart Won't Let Go
Includes the strongholds of Addiction, Doubt, Unbelief, Failure, Fear, Idolatry, Image, Impurity, Independence, Divorce, and Religiosity.

When the Heart Won't Let Go
Workbook

When the Heart Won't Let Go

Breaking Negative Patterns Series
Book II

*The Step-by-Step Manual to
Releasing the Heart from Stress
and Moving Beyond Grief,
Hurt, and Anxiety*

Lisa Tyson

A Gold Lantern Media Publication

© 2019 by Gold Lantern Media

Pages of this book may be reproduced in order to help others identify and break strongholds. Scanning, uploading, and distributing via the internet without permission is illegal.

Negative Patterns Identifications Form © Gold Lantern Media

Scripture quotations are taken from the Authorized *King James Version* of the Bible.

Published by
Gold Lantern Media
P.O. Box 208
Nine Mile Falls, Wa 99026
Printed in the United States of America
For Worldwide Distribution
www.goldlanternmedia.com

Cover Design: Laura Tyson

This book is dedicated to my five- gallon bucket friend, Corey Skinner. Your optimism and joy are a constant reminder to me of God's love for me. Your tender heart and ability to carry the burdens of others is an amazing example to the world.
I experienced my own personal sorrow and grief as I studied and wrote about the healing of it. During this time, you faithfully prayed for me and uplifted me in my dark season of the soul. Your support through one of the most stressful years of my life has been comforting, genuine, and selfless. You've consistently reminded me that Jesus was the greatest burden bearer of all time. He went through deep grief as He carried the sins and burdens of the world. You are leaving your mark in a powerful and moving way and I am forever grateful.

Contents

Seasons of Life
1. *What's Happening?* Understanding Seasons   1
2. No Water in the Pit *Joseph's Seasons*   7
3. The Big Picture   13
4. The Stress Test *Acknowledging Stress in Each Season*   15

We all Experience Loss
5. Expressions of Loss   21
6. Your True Treasure is in Heaven   23
7. Buried Feelings Never Die   27
8. The Mystery of Invisible Loss   31
9. Bitter Waves   35
10. The Big Adjustment *Ripples of Invisible Loss*   39
11. All Things are Possible with God   41

Grief...It's Complicated
12. Compounded Grief *The Silent Avalanche*   45
13. Suppressions of Grief *The Don't Cry Lie*   47
14. Allie's Dilemma   49
15. Grief *The Needle in the Haystack*   53
16. Seven Signs of Hidden Grief   55
17. What do Grief Counselors Advise?   59

Soul Ties
18. Unspoken Connections   63
19. Natasha's Soul Tie   65
20. When the Heart Won't Let Go   67
21. Soul Tie *Q & A*   71

Burden Bearing
22. The Five-Gallon Bucket Person — 75
23. Understand It — 77
24. Points of Caution — 79
25. Obedience is Better than Sacrifice — 83
26. Training for the Burden Bearer — 85

Preparation for Healing
27. Healing of the Heart in Hebrew Culture — 89
28. I'm Ready to Process my Grief *What Can I Expect?* — 95
29. Seven Steps to Healing — 97
30. Anointing with Oil — 99

Let's Do It! Layers of Healing
31. Stronghold Breaking — 101
32. Seven Steps to Breaking Soul Ties — 107
33. The Path of Light *The Beauty of Inner Healing* — 109
34. Deliverance *Q & A* — 113
35. Physical Healing *Q & A* — 119
36. Maintaining Healing *Seven Ways to Stay Free* — 121

Seven Life-Changing Prayers
37. Listening Prayer — 123
38. The Protection Prayer — 125
39. The Soul Tie Prayers — 127
40. The Inner Healing Prayer — 133
41. The Deliverance Prayer — 135
42. The Physical Healing Prayer — 139
43. The Stronghold Breaking Prayer — 141

Strongholds
- 44. ADDICTION — 143
- 45. DOUBT & UNBELIEF — 149
- 46. FAILURE — 151
- 47. FEAR — 155
- 48. IDOLATRY — 161
- 49. IMAGE — 165
- 50. IMPURITY — 169
- 51. INDEPENDENCE & DIVORCE — 171
- 52. LOSS & PROLONGED GRIEF — 173
- 53. NEGATIVITY — 179
- 54. RELIGIOSITY — 181
- Negative Pattern Identification Form

It's no accident that this information is in your hands. This indispensable reference is the second in the Breaking Negative Patterns series and is geared for anyone serious about getting free or setting others free. It builds upon the concepts of obtaining personal freedom and taking control of your destiny. These resources deal with heart issues that affect our stress levels, our emotions, and our functioning ability. They visit a variety of components, including stronghold breaking, inner healing, and soul tie breaking and they are must-reads if you've ever experienced loss or sense a calling to help others with their greatest struggles and pain. These resources also have matching workbooks which can be helpful for studying, journaling, processing, and healing.
K.S- Reading, Pennsylvania

Having struggled with emotional bondage and physical addictions, these tools were exactly what I needed to learn how to submit issues daily and break free from them. Being adopted and not knowing what was in my family history, this material helped me walk through each step of healing and gain freedom, as I've learned to submit and confess each time something may arise. The books in the *Breaking Negative Patterns Series* would be a great study for women's and men's ministries, including recovery ministries. I could also see it being used as an amazing tool for premarital counseling. Honestly, there are no limitations on how or where you may desire to use it. The one thing I love is that the strategies have become ingrained into my daily life and I am able to take a real assessment of areas I am struggling with and break free from them. I am so encouraged, as it has taken me years to move past some of my hurts, hang-ups, stresses, and addictions.

The author has made this an easy read with a lifetime worth of tools in the palm of your hand. Love it... If you are struggling, or know someone who is, it will help you break through and experience true freedom! The tools that are in this series truly changed my life.
C. J- Fort Wayne, Indiana

This book is amazing. It will challenge your thinking and help you understand the reason you are trapped in your negative patterns. If you want to be free from years of negative patterns, I highly recommend the series. Once you understand the power of being set free you will want to share it with everyone!
S.G- Reynoldsburg, Ohio

I don't even know how to explain this experience. It's the guide I didn't know I needed! I've struggled for a long time with anxiety and depression. Every time I felt like I was moving forward, I would get sucked back again. But this isn't like that...This guide is something completely different! Even the way it came into my life, through a chance meeting with Lisa, just reaffirms to me how much more is out there! I've only just started the process of breaking negative patterns and strongholds, but already it has been incredibly meaningful, energizing, and transformative! I can't explain it, but this was a very powerful experience for me. I FELT something. I went THROUGH something. I felt release, and energy, and HEALING. And I can't wait for more!!!
J.B- Lompoc, Ca

A Note to the Reader

Just like you, I've had trouble balancing rest and staying whole through the confusing seasons of life. Whether you're reading this series to become better equipped to help others, or you are on a journey to experiencing a new awareness and freedom, allow this material to help you identify what's inside your heart. Utilize this book as well as the matching workbook, as a guide to understanding the stresses of loss, and as a resource to offer hope to others.

When the Heart Won't Let Go is the second book in the *Breaking Negative Patterns Series.* Within these pages, you'll come across patterns of the number seven multiple times. As I was writing, it simply happened to show itself. In the book, *Numbers That Preach,* we learn that the number seven marks where God is doing something by His Spirit apart from any other source. *Seven is perfection of Spirit.* It's the number that marks God's rest; where He rules over all things created. It was the most sacred number to the Hebrews and they recognized seven as a pattern, given by God from the very beginning.[1]

I have tried to take a complex subject and put it into simple, concrete terms. It's my sincere hope that you, the reader, will appreciate the healing solutions offered and incorporate them as powerful tools now, and throughout the rest of your life.

---

[1] Brewer, T. A., *Numbers That Preach* (Aventine Press, 2007), p 87

Seasons of Life

1

What's Happening?
Understanding Seasons

In the same way that we have seasons in nature, there are seasons that we go through in life. They are invisible, but if we become sensitive to them, we can flow with them instead of against them.

When I was a little girl, one of the hardest concepts for me to grasp was the concept of natural seasons. Growing up in California, the sun shone year round. I had been sheltered from frigid winters. Fall passed pretty quickly each year and spring usually started early. It wasn't until I was nineteen years old that it clicked.

It was January 1998. I had just driven with my dad from California to World Harvest Bible College in Columbus, Ohio. I made friends quickly and remember them asking me if I was comfortable in my white heels and long, thin skirts. I had arrived in the dead of winter, and it was *cold*.

After a few weeks of freezing and a small car accident on black ice, I quickly learned to adapt to the changes that came with the season of winter and began to watch my calendar in anticipation of spring. I also started to become more aware of mentally preparing for seasons. I didn't want to be caught off guard again. We can be jolted into a new season unexpectedly when an accident or injury changes our routine. Other times, there are signposts that give us clues that change is on the horizon.

In the spring of 2008, I was joyfully working as an elementary teacher in Southern California. I was enjoying my role as an administrative assistant, a soccer coach, and elementary teacher. My life felt perfect. I was passionate about the people in my life and my career. I enjoyed success in my daily achievement and saw that I was inspiring the next generation.

When the school year ended in June, I was shocked to hear that my school assignment was changing. The district needed me across the street at the junior high. My heart was breaking as I pondered leaving the staff and students I had grown to love. Nothing in me wanted to let go of the familiarity, the relationships, and the bonds that I had created. I put it out of mind all summer.

The new school year was looming, and I knew the move was inevitable. I waited until the last moment of summer to move into my new classroom, hoping for a miracle, praying, and believing God that something would change. However, there was no change. A few days before school began, I started my year with prayer. I was sitting in my living room in our comfy, blue La-Z-Boy chair.

My eyes were closed as I waited on the Lord. I have found that when I close my eyes and pray, I see images in my mind. I don't always understand them, but I try. During that prayer time, I was able to see or sense the next few months ahead. It looked like a path that I felt represented the next season until approximately the middle of December. After that point, I sensed there was a block. The block was like a black fog that started at the end of the path. I concluded that the Lord wanted me to focus on the few months ahead of me and not worry about anything beyond that time.

The next few months were strange. Many of my new junior high students had a family member in jail. They seemed distant compared to my elementary students. They stole things off of my desk, complained about our procedures, and were confrontational. It was stressful and each day seemed like three.

I was still grieving the loss of my last season, and driving by my prior students playing on the playground across the street, was like pouring salt in my wounds. I felt like I was suffering, yet I never lost my peace. In Romans 5 we read, *"Therefore being justified by faith, we have peace with God through our Lord Jesus Christ: By whom also we have access by faith into this grace wherein we stand, and rejoice in hope of the glory of God. And not only so, but we glory in tribulations also: knowing that tribulation worketh patience; And patience, experience; and experience, hope: And hope maketh not ashamed; because the love of God is shed abroad in our hearts by the Holy Ghost which is given unto us."*

Even though God's Word reminds us that we are to glory in tribulations because they work in us patience, experience, and hope, it's not easy. About eight weeks into the school year, I remember having an urge to pack up my closets at home. I started thinking about consolidating my belongings into little boxes and felt an urgency to pack up our house. It made no sense, and I didn't follow the promptings.

Fast forward to the end of Christmas break. I was visiting family in Texas when I received a phone call from a school in Australia. A Christian school had heard of my teaching and wanted to offer me an interview for a teaching job starting immediately. I prayed about it with my family, and we felt peace. I agreed to a phone interview and they asked if I'd be available on a day that I'd be returning to California on back to back flights.

In my heart I reflected to the Lord... *If this is You, let the interview call come while I'm available and my phone has service.* I wanted confirmation. I'd be flying between six to eight hours that day with two layovers, and Australia was eighteen hours ahead. Connecting for the interview could be a challenge and God would need to work out all the details to show me that this was from Him. *Malachi 3:10 says, "Prove me now herewith, saith the Lord of hosts, if I will not open you the windows of heaven, and pour you out a blessing, that there shall not be room enough to receive it."*

The day of the interview, my husband and I caught our first flight. There were no missed calls and no messages. We arrived and went to the terminal to wait for our second flight. We boarded and arrived in California that evening. We landed and gathered our belongings from the overhead storage bins. I turned my phone on and began to leave the plane. It was just then, inside the gangway boarding bridge that it began to ring. I looked at my husband and then looked at my phone and identified the lengthy number as an international call. He took our bags and disappeared while I sat down to answer.

The airport was humming with sound. I covered my left ear and answered the phone. Over the next little while, I responded to questions and began to feel in my heart that I would get the job. My season was about to change!

On the way home from the airport, I planted seeds in my husband's heart that we needed to consider preparing and getting ready. I knew it was all happening a little fast for him, but at the same time, the past few months were starting to make sense. Sure enough, a couple of days later, I was hired and was given two weeks to arrive. I would be starting the school year late, but they would cover me with another teacher.

I happily gave my two-week notice and was relieved when the human resource clerk secretly shared that she also would leave her job for an adventure in Australia. I began to see the Lord's hand in the painful season shift over the past summer. I would never have wanted to leave the elementary school where I had been teaching. He allowed me to grieve the season as I tried to let go, and put me through a short season of discomfort at the junior high so that when He called me to Australia, I would jump in with open arms.

Two weeks later, as my plane landed in Rockhampton, Australia, I remember thinking that it looked like paradise. I could see the tranquil, turquoise ocean mixed with navy blue. The palm trees swayed in the breeze, and I was delighted to find that the entire school had come to the airport in busses to greet me with cheery smiles and welcome signs.

I was overwhelmed with love and thrilled to be starting my new assignment. Looking back, I was stepping into one of the most amazing seasons of my life.

2

No Water in the Pit
Joseph's Seasons

Joseph was raised in his father's home and was born into favor because of who his mother was. His ten older half-brothers knew that Joseph was especially loved, and began to harbor seeds of hatred, as Joseph shared detailed stories with their father of what his brothers were doing in the fields.

He was a gifted young man with a tender heart and began to receive prophetic revelation through dreams at a very early age. Joseph was learning to operate in the invisible "Kingdom" culture, where the dreams of prophetic vision are not often tangible at their conception.

Joseph was making a serious sacrifice in the innocent sharing of his dreams, and each bit of revelation he shared with his brothers increased the tension. Their small minds did not understand Kingdom culture.

As Joseph shared, Satan heard the vision as well and devised jealousy and animosity in the hearts of his brothers to abort the dream. Joseph's life was about to resemble a roller coaster, a wild ride of experiences that would develop his character and ultimately lead him to come full circle. The enemy was plotting to destroy Joseph; however, God had other plans. He would need to be removed and tried and then positioned to save the very brothers who were about to betray him.

The familiarity in Joseph's world was about to come to an end. God knew it would be impossible for Joseph to fulfill his destiny in the tiny, comfortable hometown he had been raised in. When Joseph went to visit his brothers, at the request of their father, they saw him coming in the distance and devised a plan. They threw him into a pit where he was left in solitude. It must have been a confusing and heartbreaking trauma for the teenager. The Bible says there was no water in the pit (Genesis 37:24); and his brothers referred to him as having anguish of soul (Genesis 42:21).

Some seasons can cause wounds. The trauma of being thrown into the pit and sold (betrayed by family) is what I refer to as a "dark season of the soul." *Trauma* represents the robbery of something by someone. It is a loss of the worst kind. It involves a lack of love, which can create soul wounds. These wounds grieve the heart and can cause a broken spirit. It leaves an imprint and can produce many tears. Joseph's betrayal robbed him of the family security he had always known, rendering him helpless and wounding him deeply.

Amid the betrayal, he was sold into slavery and permanently lost the life he had known. All of his familiar comforts were taken in an instant: his family, his work, his belongings, his culture, his language, his religion, and his friends. Joseph experienced a profound loss of many kinds all at once; This is referred to as *compounded loss*. The isolated season of pruning had begun.

We know that in the tumultuous times ahead, God would be with Joseph (Genesis 39:2, 21). Midianite merchantmen on camels purchased Joseph from the pit. They took him to Egypt and sold him to Potiphar's house and it was there that Joseph began to operate in his calling of leadership and ministry. He started to find favor in new positions of authority.

During this time, Joseph served and labored for Potiphar for years, building relationships and experiencing blissful seasons of success. Running Potiphar's house was preparation for administrating for Pharaoh, one of the most powerful men in the world. However, in the midst of his success, Joseph plummeted into a season of testing.

Without warning, he was tempted in the palace by Potiphar's wife, but proved his integrity, standing steadfast in loyalty to Potiphar, to God, and to himself. He experienced a season of "dying-to-self" as he maintained his integrity, passing through the testing season of temptation with flying colors. God was developing in him restraint, discretion, and wisdom.

Wrongly accused by Potiphar's wife, he was catapulted yet into another undeserved and deep valley. This false accusation robbed Joseph of his position in Potiphar's house. It must have been excruciating being wrongfully accused, removed from authority, isolated, and imprisoned. The future looked bleak.

We know Joseph was in prison for more than two years (Genesis 41:1). During this season Joseph didn't even look like himself (Genesis 41:14). He may have questioned if all of his work in Potiphar's house had been a failure. Day after day as Joseph slowly passed the time, you can be sure Satan was in his ear, reminding him of his excessive losses and reflecting blame and accusation toward God for the injustice. Joseph kept his head up and focused on the task at hand.

In prison, Joseph's leadership qualities earned him another position of trust and responsibility, as he became the leader of the other inmates. He continued to use the gifts God had given him, even in the prison dungeon. Joseph's humiliating experience of loss continued as disappointment set in after he interpreted the baker and butler's dream three days before Pharaoh's birthday. At this time, he was promised the chief butler would give him a good word, but then was forgotten.

The enemy's plan is to disorient us in our darkest seasons. His ultimate plan is to destroy our lives. Imagine if Joseph had given up, given in, and taken his own life. If Joseph could just persevere through the trials, God would surely restore him and replace all that had been stolen. Joseph simply had to trust in God's timing.

Even though Joseph couldn't see it, God was using these difficult seasons to prepare him for his future. Joseph had walked through the ups and downs and had held onto his faith. He kept a positive attitude of trust, knowing that God was on his side and had destined him with purpose. His faith was built in the face of adversity, as he moved forward through each hardship.

Everything was falling into place. Joseph was right where he was supposed to be. God had positioned him perfectly for the upcoming famine. He was in Egypt as a deliverer, to preserve the house of Israel.

At thirty years of age, Joseph experienced an instant breakthrough. God had paved the way for him to interpret Pharaoh's dream. God also gave him a plan, so that when he stood before Pharaoh, he found favor. Overnight, Joseph instantly was promoted to position, wealth, and power (Genesis 41:42). He literally stepped into a new life. He was given a new job, a new name, new clothes, and a wife.

Within five years his wife had borne him two sons. Joseph called the name of the firstborn Manasseh which means *"For God hath made me forget all my toil, and all my father's house"* (Genesis 41:51). The name of the second son he called Ephraim which means *"For God hath caused me to be fruitful in the land of my affliction."* (Genesis 41:52)

After the years of plenty, the seven-year famine started and Joseph's brothers soon came to Egypt to get help. At this point, Joseph entered a season of clarity. He understood that God had placed him in Egypt with purpose. Incredibly, he had forgiven his brothers; however, when he saw them, they did not immediately have his trust. They needed to rebuild it, and he gave them that opportunity.

On their second trip, after a couple of stressful months, Joseph shared his true identity with his brothers. Read Genesis 45:1-11 and watch how the story comes full circle. The end of the story involves a sweet and refreshing season for Joseph. He brought his entire family to Egypt to live close to him, and Pharaoh gave them the best land in Goshen. His father lived an additional seventeen years, and his family and their cattle grew exponentially, populating the whole region.

I love how Joseph was able to see the big picture. He did not hold bitterness or contempt in his heart toward his brothers. Joseph's story can help us to acknowledge seasons and acknowledging them can help us to see the big picture.

3

The Big Picture

Often in the high seasons we forget that we ever experienced the low seasons. In the low seasons, things can be so low that everything appears bleak and hopeless. The list below includes a variety of seasons, many of which Joseph experienced.

By no means is the list comprehensive; in fact, you may want to add to it from your own personal experience. Revisit the following list of seasons in the future to shine clarity on your circumstances.

   Season of Accusation
   Season of Betrayal
   Season of Character Growth and Development
   Season of Change
   Season of Clarity
   Season of Disappointment
   Season of Dying-to-Self
   Season of Favor
   Season of Faith Building
   Season of Hope Deferred
   Season of Humility

Season of Infirmity
Season of Labor
Season of Leadership & Authority
Season of Loss, Grief, Sadness, and Sorrow "The dark season of the soul"
Season of Ministry
Season of Obedience
Season of New Beginnings
Season of Perceived Failure
Season of Preparation
Season of Promise and Destiny
Season of Prophetic Revelation
Season of Pruning
Season of Refreshing
Season of Restoration
Season of Solitude
Season of Success
Season of Surrender
Season of Temptation
Season of Testing
Season of the Valley
Season of Victory

4

The Stress Test
Acknowledging Stress in Each Season

Stress begins when something uncomfortable happens or is happening. Whenever someone feels forced to do or deal with something that they'd rather not, there is an element of discomfort that arises. Physiologically, the neurological system is heightened and creates a chain reaction of responses in the brain and body.

As the discomfort continues, the body begins to adapt through neurological and physiological change. In some seasons, long term stress may become familiar, which can damage the body, causing early aging, adrenal fatigue, and disease. Additionally, loss and discomfort from other areas can compound, generating to acute levels.

In 1967, two psychiatrists Thomas Holmes and Richard Rahe examined the medical records of over 5,000 patients, as a way to determine whether stressful events could cause illnesses. Patients were asked to tally a list of life events based on a relative score. Rahe tested the reliability of the stress scale again in 1970. He gave the scale to 2,500 US Navy seamen and had them rank their most stressful life events. The sailors were then tracked for six months. Their visits to the dispensary were logged, to find if there were correlations between their reported "life stress" and their visits to the doctor.

Thomas Holmes and Richard Rahe found that a strong correlation did exist. It was so strong that they found the more stressful the event, the higher the likelihood of illness. A score of 300 or higher put a person at risk of illness; 150-299 showed moderate risk and a score of less than 150 predicted only a slight risk of illness.

These results were published as *The Holmes and Rahe Stress Scale.* It is currently used by many doctors to better understand the effects of stressful events on the body. You'll notice that quite a few of the events listed are actually *losses*, such as a separation in a relationship.

Q: Can a loss be disguised as stress?

A: Yes. There are certain types of loss which can slip by unnoticed and go unprocessed. They can accumulate in the body, presenting as extreme stress.

Loss can be understood by seeing it as the *removal of familiarity*. In our culture, loss is attributed most commonly to someone's passing. However, the truth is that the loss of anything important, anything of value, can cause grief.

Additionally, grieving can occur over a *perceived* loss. In the Bible, Abraham (the Father of Faith) and his wife

Sarah grieved over not having children. In Genesis 11:30 we read that Sarah was barren; she had no child and in Genesis 15:2-3 Abraham complains to God for lack of an heir.

Following is a list of the most stressful life events according to *The Holmes And Rahe Stress Scale*. Each event is assigned a *Life Change Unit* score. For purposes of assisting the reader in recognizing loss, the letter (L) is tagged to the end of life events that can be considered a "loss."

The Stress Test

Acknowledging loss gives the heart permission to grieve. To take this test, tally the points of each life event which has affected you personally over the past year. The final score will reveal how impactful your current stress levels are on your health.

Life Event	Life Change Units
Death of a spouse (L)	100
Divorce (L)	73
Marital separation (L)	65
Imprisonment (L)	63
Death of close family member (L)	63
Personal injury or illness (L)	53
Marriage	50
Dismissal from work (L)	47
Marital reconciliation	45
Retirement (L)	45
Health change in family member	44
Pregnancy	40

Sexual difficulties	39
The gain of a new family member	39
Business readjustment	39
Change in financial state (L)	38
Death of a close friend (L)	37
Change to a different line of work	36
Change in frequency of arguments	35
Major mortgage accumulation	32
Foreclosure of a mortgage loan (L)	30
Responsibility change at work	29
A child leaving home (L)	29
Trouble with in-laws	29
Outstanding personal achievement	28
Spouse starting or stopping work	26
Beginning or ending school (L)	26
Change in living conditions	25
Revision of personal habits	24
Troubles with boss	23
Change in working hours or conditions	20
Change in residence (L)	20
Change in schools (L)	20
Change in recreation	19
Change in church activities	19
Change in social activities	18
Minor mortgage or loan	17
Change in sleeping habits	16
Change in number of family reunions	15
Change in eating habits	15
Vacation	13
Major holiday	12
Minor violation of law	11

Score of 300+: High risk of illness
Score of 150-299: Moderate risk of illness (reduced by 30% from the above risk)
Score <150: Slight risk of illness

Stress and Non-Adults

Non-adults are less able to cope with stressful events and need more assistance to navigate stressful times. The scale was modified for non-adults and is scored in the same way:

Life Event	Life Change Units
Death of a parent (L)	100
Unplanned pregnancy/abortion (L)	100
Getting married	95
Divorce of parents (L)	90
Acquiring a visible deformity (L)	80
Fathering a child	70
Jail sentence of a parent over one year (L)	70
Marital separation of parents (L)	69
Death of a brother or sister (L)	68
Change in acceptance by peers (L)	67
Unplanned pregnancy of sister	64
Death of a close friend (L)	63
The marriage of a parent to stepparent (L)	63
Discovery of being adopted (L)	63
Having a visible congenital deformity	62
Serious illness requiring hospitalization	58
Failure of a grade in school	56
Hospitalization of a parent	55
Breakup with a boyfriend or girlfriend (L)	53
Jail sentence of parent over 30 days (L)	53

Beginning to date	51
Becoming involved with drugs or alcohol	50
Birth of a brother or sister	50
Suspension from school	50
Increase in arguments between parents	47
Outstanding personal achievement	46
Loss of job by parent	46
Change in parent's financial status	45
Acceptance at a college of choice	43
Being a senior in high school	42
Hospitalization of a sibling	41
Increased absence of a parent from home	38
Brother or sister leaving home (L)	37
Addition of a third adult to the family	34
Becoming a member of a church	31
A decrease in arguments between parents	27
Mother or father beginning work	26
Decrease in arguments with parents	26

We all Experience Loss

5

Expressions of Loss

"He healeth the broken in heart, and bindeth up their wounds." (Psalms 147:3)

Six Expressions of Loss:

1. The state or fact of being rendered nonexistent, physically unsound, or useless.
Synonyms: demolition, extermination, extinction
Related Words: collapse, disintegration, dissolution
Near Antonyms: preservation, restoration
Antonyms: construction, raising

2. A person or thing harmed, lost, or destroyed.
Synonyms: casualty, fatality, victim
Related Words: collateral damage
Near Antonym: victor

3. Failure to win a contest.
Synonym: defeat
Related Words: failure, flop
Near Antonyms: accomplishment, achievement
Antonyms: success, triumph, victory

4. Loss of value or the amount by which something is lessened.
Synonyms: decline, decrease, depletion, reduction
Related Words: deduction, subtraction
Near Antonym: accumulation
Antonyms: gain, increase

5. The act or an instance of not having or being able to find.
Synonym: misplacement
Related Word: lack
Antonym: recovery

6. Trauma; The state of being robbed of something familiar or normally enjoyed.
Synonym: deprivation
Related Word: absence
Near Antonym: possession

6

Your True Treasure is in Heaven

"Lay not up for yourselves treasures upon earth, where moth and rust doth corrupt, and where thieves break through and steal: But lay up for yourselves treasures in heaven, where neither moth nor rust doth corrupt, and where thieves do not break through nor steal: For where your treasure is, there will your heart be also." (Matthew 6:19-21)

My Story...

On the night of November 1, 2005, my husband and I were in Westlake Village, California, attending a healing training workshop with friends and family. We had borrowed my in-law's van and had taken my dad, brother, and two friends with us. After experiencing a long and powerful night of singing, healing, and spiritual freedom, we headed home.

Around 11:45 pm we were driving east, into the Antelope Valley headed towards Littlerock, California. Less than ten miles from home, we saw huge flames, and concluded that someone's yard was on fire.

Our curiosity moved us faster toward home. As we approached, our anxiety heightened exponentially, as we realized the fire was on our street. Pulling up we were in shock; it was our house that was burning down! We jumped out of the van, and I dialed 911, wondering where help was with a fire station only two blocks away.

We opened the gate and realized that along with our home, our truck and our car were melting and there was nothing we could do. Our entire house was in flames. I stood back in shock, trying to control my heart rate. For the next two hours, we stared speechless, as firefighters put out the blaze. Everything was gone.

It was after two am. I was laying on my in-law's couch in a fog, numb and struggling to sleep. Very clearly, my spirit received a message from the Lord that I've never forgotten. The words were few, but they were crystal clear. *Your true treasure is in heaven.*

I instantly had a shift in my perception and realized that all of the material things that I had lost were just that... material. I began to give gratitude to God for saving our lives. I gave thanks that we did not have any pets who could have died, and that we weren't sleeping in the house when it started.

I began to realize that in the big scheme of things, the real value was in the people who were in my life. After I was reminded that *my true treasures were in heaven*, it removed the high value that I had placed on material things, a lesson that has since stayed with me.

I remember waking up November 2nd, realizing that I didn't have a toothbrush, hairbrush, or shampoo. I was processing the concept that we were completely starting over. Later, we had two investigators who came out separately to inspect the property; one believed that the fire had started on the northeast corner and the other thought that it had started on the southwest corner. Neither of them could give us any answers.

We were very blessed after the fire by an outpouring of compassion from members of our church and community. Within less than a week, we were offered countless vehicles to borrow and places to stay. Over seven thousand dollars was gifted to us in the first few days to help us start fresh. Agape love was shown to us in the form of utensils, pillows, clothing, gift cards, and more.

One of my favorite memories is of a blanket that my friend Carolyn gave me after the house burned down. Each night during the cold months that followed, I pulled it tightly to my chin before I fell asleep and was reminded of the beautiful, comforting love of God.

Never had I experienced the Body of Christ operate as the hands of God in such a powerful and personal way. To this day, we continue to be incredibly grateful and humbled by the love that was so selflessly shown to us in one of our darkest seasons.

Survival Mode

One vivid morning a few days after our home had burned down, I was driving south on California's 14 Freeway. My mind was empty; I felt numb and was on autopilot, as I got off at the exit to the Palmdale Mall. As I came down the ramp I got into the left turn lane and focused on the car ahead of me. We both turned left across the intersection, and as I looked up, it was clear I was running a very red light. The traffic had already started across the road, and the first car in line was a Highway Patrol. I locked eyes with him, realizing what was happening, and desperately hoping I could be invisible for the next ten seconds. His siren blared as he pulled me to the side of the road.

I couldn't believe I had blatantly run a red light. I was grateful I hadn't been in an accident, but my lack of focus and attention was concerning to me. I wondered what was wrong with me. I apologized profusely to the officer and told him I must not be feeling myself because of the house burning down a few days before. He said he understood and was sorry, but he'd need to to give me a ticket.

Afterward, I remember sitting in the vehicle with my head on the steering wheel losing the fight to hold back tears. I found myself experiencing physical and emotional expressions of grief, not realizing that I had just suffered a deep loss and that my thoughts and feelings (the beginnings of grief) were a result of the profound and recent loss in my life.

At the time, I didn't know that a loss could come without losing a loved one. I didn't realize that I was starting to process. I didn't understand what was happening to me, but I was learning a valuable lesson. *Before I could cope with my loss, I first had to acknowledge it.*

7

Buried Feelings Never Die

"Time does not heal all wounds. I heal all wounds."

In the weeks after our house burned down, I found solace in quiet time spent with the Lord. We were staying with our friends, Bill and Sandy Balch, in Palmdale, California. Each day, after everyone left for work, I would lay prostrate on the living room floor, picturing myself laying before God's throne.

I had lost everything. I felt empty, broken, and desolate. I would come to the Lord this way, sobbing until there were no tears left to cry. I would get glimpses of Him and His love. I know that the Bible tells us that no man has ever seen God, and I don't claim that I have, but I do believe I have seen His feet while I was laying there and His hands and arms as He picked me up. I have felt His chest as He cradled me against Himself in comfort. I remember hearing Him whisper to me, *"Time does not heal all wounds. I heal all wounds."*

It was during these times that I experienced His profound tenderness in a way I had never known. Through these experiences, I was acknowledging and processing our loss and trying to move forward. When I was out, I found myself talking with others about what had happened and sharing my thoughts and emotions openly.

My husband, Eli was drawn to the scene of the fire and would dig through the remains with a spoon. He kept his feelings and emotions to himself, barely sharing his thoughts with me. He occasionally would find a remnant of an object that had held value and would present it to me, but I just wasn't interested. I was not curious about the charred remains or interested in searching at the site of the fire.

Although I did spend a short time trying to clean some of the items Eli found, I really didn't want the reminder of what we had lost. I felt that there was nothing of value left in the black rubble (at least, nothing that I wanted to take with me into our next season).

No two people grieve alike, and I was beginning to realize that my husband and I were dealing with our losses in different ways. We had been married for five years and had never shared a loss up to that point.

About a month after the house burned down, Eli and I were eating out with friends and he passed out. His face and lips turned white as he fell against my shoulder. At first, I thought he was joking until I saw his color.

Steve Hunter, one of our dinner friends, happened to be an EMT (emergency medical technician). He immediately jumped up to the edge of the table, asking questions about

Eli's health. *Was he diabetic? Was he hypoglycemic?* At the time I had no idea what those words meant and didn't know how to answer. I felt helpless.

A woman from a neighboring table quickly offered orange juice, which we dabbed on his mouth. Time seemed to stand still. In what felt like an eternity, Eli came to. We later learned that Eli was hypoglycemic, and hadn't eaten anything since the day before. We spent that night in the emergency room, with Eli connected to an IV. They found a darkened room for him, and I remember cuddling with him all night on an awkward hospital gurney to keep him warm. Sadly, this event began a domino effect of serious health problems for him.

In the months following, Eli's health teetered on the edge. His blood sugar swung drastically several times per day. He was exhausted continually and felt faint and dizzy. I quickly learned to cook balancing blood sugar meals, which the doctor ordered he eat five times per day. The *compounded stress* was taking its toll on both of us.

In meeting with our family friend and naturopath, Dr. Emard, he explained that the fire had caused us deep stress which was being exaggerated by grief. Instead of expressing and processing the feelings, my husband had held them all inside. We learned that internal stress had drained Eli's adrenals. If not handled, it could turn into *prolonged grief* (living in a lengthy state of despair) and could bring his health to ruin.

We began to see that our bodies are designed to be a processing plant. Just as they process the food we eat, they process feelings that we experience from events. Without expressing the feelings, they compound.

Through this discussion, my husband was able to identify his feelings. He was angry and sad that he had lost his tools, and he was frustrated that he didn't have the chance to save our scrapbooks and other valuable belongings.

Eli confessed holding on to anger, sadness, and frustration. *Why?* The Bible tells us to "cast our cares upon the Lord." When we hold onto them, they can become too heavy. The Bible also tells us in James 5:16 that if we confess our faults one to another, that *we will be healed.* Our bodies were meant to *process* rather than *store,* and processing often occurs through tears. Tears are our body's way of cleansing. Soon after releasing the burdens, Eli began to heal.

We began to start each day with prayer and a fruit smoothie and began a health protocol of supplements. It took my husband's body awhile to heal (over eighteen months) but it finally did and he regained his health. It *is* possible to be successful in moving forward after loss.

We realized after the fire that unprocessed feelings bring damage to the body. Through our loss, we learned a valuable lesson. *Not allowing the heart to acknowledge and process what it's feeling, can cost a person a lot in the long run.*

8

The Mystery of Invisible Loss

"Many are the afflictions of the righteous: but the Lord delivereth him out of them all." (Psalm 34:19)

Loss can be hard to identify. It's like a colorful ball of yarn. Imagine the emotion of grief as a blue string. The event of a loss as a green string, the shock of trauma as a red string, and the injury of abuse as a purple string. Compound that with adding the colors black, orange, pink, and white to represent symptoms of grief, coping with loss, understanding feelings, and the difference between grief and loss.

The aim is to unravel the colors and make sense of some of the most misunderstood and undervalued feelings and emotions that we will ever encounter. To identify invisible loss, we must first understand visible loss.

Below is a list of common visible losses. <u>The numbers next to each visible loss correlate to the different expressions of loss in chapter five</u>. There is "visible loss" that occurs through a physical experience or event such as:

* Loss of Human Life of someone we valued (1)
* Divorce (1)
* Loss of a Business (1)
* Loss of Home due to a sale or other reasons (1)
* Loss of a Pet (1)
* Loss through Disaster (1)

Visible losses are relatively obvious to our circle of influence (family, friends, acquaintances) and receive acknowledgment and support unless the loss was quietly kept private.

Less acknowledged, but just as powerful, is "invisible loss." We can experience invisible losses which can compound (multiples of imperceptible loss at the same time) especially after a *visible* loss. Without realizing it, a visible loss can be the trigger that creates an avalanche effect, opening file folders which represent years of compounded and *unacknowledged* invisible loss.

Invisible losses tend to go unacknowledged and are often kept private. This type of grief can be powerfully hard, as the support of those we love may be faint as they struggle to decipher our feelings.

The following losses represent a sampling of the many, many types of invisible losses that can happen to someone. Again, the number next to each loss correlates to the *definitions* of loss in chapter five. In no way do they depict a value to the loss, as losses cannot be compared.

* Loss of a Baby through miscarriage or stillbirth (1)
* Abortion (1)
* Loss of a Body Part through accident or disease (2)
* Loss of Trust in a person who harmed us (2)
* Loss through Failure after expectation of success (3)
* Loss of Innocence (4)
* Loss of Purity (4)
* Loss of the Familiar (4)
* Romantic Loss due to breakup (4)
* Loss of a Relationship with someone we valued (4)
* Loss of the Family dynamic (4)
* Loss of a Lifestyle (4)
* Loss of perceived wholeness through a changed Role (spouse, father, mother, sister, brother, granddaughter, grandson, friend, caregiver) (4)
* Loss of a Support system (4)
* Loss of Value for Traditions (4)
* Loss of Career through Retirement or other (5)
* Loss of Identity (5)
* Loss of Dreams (5)
* Missed Opportunities (5)
* Loss of a Sense of Purpose (5)
* Loss of Direction (5)
* Loss of Confidence (5)
* Loss of Faith (5)
* Loss of Hope (5)
* Loss of Motivation (5)
* Loss through Betrayal or being lied to(6)
* Perceived Loss (5)
* Loss through Realization that your reality is different from someone else's (5)

* Loss of Self (perceived identity) through weight gain, injury, or something else (5)
* Loss of Self that's been given to another in love (5)
* Loss through Heartbreak (6)
* Loss of Income or Financial security (6)
* Loss in an Accident where another was at fault (6)
* Loss from a Loved one's Suicide (6)
* Loss of Security or feeling Safe (6)
* Loss of a proper and functional Childhood (6)
* Loss of Purity through it being Stolen (6)
* Loss through being the Victim of a Crime (6)
* Loss of Health through physical Assault (6)
* Loss of Innocence through Abuse (6)
* Loss through Home Invasion (6)
* Loss of a Passion or Job due to Abuse, Accusation or Injustice (6)

If you are currently experiencing loss, visible or invisible, know that we have a loving Father. Our culture tells us that time heals all wounds, but the truth is that *God heals all wounds*.

9

Bitter Waves

"The LORD is nigh unto them that are of a broken heart; and saveth such as be of a contrite spirit. Many are the afflictions of the righteous: but the LORD delivereth him out of them all." (Psalm 34:18-19)

Nicole married her high school sweetheart and gave birth to their first baby when she was very young. Within the early hours at the hospital, the newborn was diagnosed with a severe lung infection. Nicole and her husband experienced a lot of anxiety during this time. A few days later, while still in the hospital, their little girl unexpectedly passed away.

The Bible uses the word "bitter" when describing the loss of the firstborn or only child. Zechariah 12:10 says *"They shall mourn for him, as one mourneth for his only son, and shall be in bitterness for him, as one that is in bitterness for his firstborn."*

Nicole and her husband were devastated. For months the two of them struggled blindly through each day. They wondered if life would ever return to normal.

Grief seemed to unfold like ocean waves that just kept crashing, as the realization of the extent of their loss set in. They became emotionally numb and struggled to find meaning in their day-to-day activities.

The disappointment of losing their first child turned to injustice. *How had this happened?* Nicole's heaviness of heart was made worse by the deep guilt she felt for not having her baby in the hospital room with her while she slept. She wrestled with deep regrets. *Could she have spent more time with the baby? Could she have done things differently? If so, how?*

The bitter grief sunk deeply in the hearts of Nicole and her husband, and it began to tear them apart. Her husband felt that he had failed somehow as a new father and blamed himself. A gloomy, dark cloud came into their lives and depression began to set in.

They no longer found joy in spending time together or nurturing their relationship. Thinking back about losing their first child, Nicole had read that many couples could be successful at working through their grief, by supporting each other through the feelings and emotion that grievers experience.

The next year, Nicole became pregnant again. She worried throughout her whole pregnancy that she would experience another loss. She didn't think she would be able to handle the pain of losing another child.

During the pregnancy she felt alone, as her husband was still dealing with the sadness and pain of losing their first. Nicole delivered a healthy baby girl and then a healthy baby boy the next year.

As time went on, Nicole's husband became more stressed and more closed off. He began to lose himself in entertainment, watching multiple television shows and movies each night, and browsing the internet regularly. Nicole felt rejected by him and his growing lack of interest in her and their children.

She felt betrayed by his checking out and began to get depressed, harboring frustration and anger at her loneliness and neglect. Neither of them were sure how to process their grief, and instead of helping each other, their pain was keeping them apart.

She knew that grief could cause withdrawal and that marriages could become extremely taxed. Nicole also knew that some marriages didn't survive the stress of the loss of a child. She began to lose hope that things would ever return to normal.

The Shock of Trauma... What Just Happened?

One morning several years later, Nicole was getting ready to run errands when she heard the Lord tell her to stay home. Since her computer screen had broken the day before, she sat down at her husband's computer to make an online order.

She opened the internet browser, and as she was typing, the address to an online dating site popped up. Confused, she followed the link. What she saw shocked her. It appeared that her husband owned an account and had a login to a website for secret affairs.

Her heart began to beat wildly, and her brain went into overdrive. Questions started to overwhelm her. *What had he done? How could he do this? How long had this been going on? Had their whole marriage been a sham? Did he love her? Was their marriage over? Was she an idiot for loving him?*

In the weeks after, Nicole uncovered her husband's darkest secrets. She used Google's activity log to research every video he had watched, every website he had visited, and every search he had made. The results were devastating. The details included dozens of searches, logs of chatting with women, and hundreds of inappropriate videos.

She also discovered years of visits to pornography websites from his computer and his phone. These had occurred multiple times per day, including while he was laying in bed next to her as she slept. She discovered that the activity had been going on since their wedding and that he'd looked for women each time he'd traveled, and even when the family had been on vacation.

His aloofness, his distraction, their arguments... it was all making sense... and the deception blew her mind. She knew that the majority of women married to husbands addicted to pornography met the criteria for Post Traumatic Stress Disorder. She wondered if she had displayed the symptoms.

10

The Big Adjustment
Ripples of Invisible Loss

The Depth and Breadth of How Loss affects us and Why we don't just "Get over It..."

For weeks, Nicole's mind was hyper-vigilant. *Where was he? Was he lying? Did she want him? Did she still love him? How could she have been such a fool?*

After finishing her research, Nicole confronted her husband with the proof. He immediately broke down in tears stating that he was happy she'd seen it all and that the exposure was lifting a heavy burden off of him. Claiming he had been keeping his addiction a secret for too long, he profusely apologized for chatting with other women and denied ever meeting anyone in person.

She struggled to forgive him as she thought back over her dedication to him and their children. She had been fiercely faithful. *Would he deceive her again? Could she ever trust him? Could their marriage truly be healed?*

Nicole's discovery of her husband's betrayal had been like a stone thrown into water. The initial shock had been the impact. The real grief was in the ripples of invisible loss that followed. Invisible loss often appears over time, rather than all at once. Those grieving may see the ripples unfold as they realize the impact that the loss has had on their everyday life.

<u>Below are three potential ripples of invisible loss that could potentially affect a person after a trauma like Nicole's:</u>

1. Loss of the known family structure: The storms of life can change the dynamic of marriage and family, creating a new level of adjustment. Additionally, grievers often feel abandoned by those they felt should have been there for them to count on, creating fresh grief over the loss of those relationships.

2. Loss of the past: Many grievers try to sum up their history and put a label on it so that it fits into a neat, little box, creating a hollow feeling of empty memories and sorrow.

3. Loss of identity: The part of the person's self that was given to another in love can feel like it is being wrenched from their being. Grievers may feel like half a person or a non-existent person. As individuals, we identify ourselves in relationships by the role or position held. When that role is no longer valid, we often lose the feeling of wholeness. Those going through grief often feel that they are losing their identity and that it is changing who they are.

11

All Things are Possible with God

"For with God nothing shall be impossible." (Luke 1:37)

Invisible losses cause disappointment, and when a person experiences betrayal at the hands of someone close to them (like Joseph), a deep wound can form. The deeper the relationship, the deeper the loss through betrayal. *"And one shall say unto him, What are these wounds in thine hands? Then he shall answer, Those with which I was wounded in the house of my friends."* (Zechariah 13:6)

Losses caused by betrayal wound our very souls. These soul wounds are invisible, but their presence can powerfully affect us internally. When this type of trauma is inflicted upon a person's heart, their soul begins to carry the weight, and may ache for the restitution of the relationship.

In a situation like Nicole's, the element of lost trust can be devastating. It can seem impossible to imagine being able to trust again. There may be fear that the future will be as painful as the present.

Nicole understood the trauma which had accompanied the shock of her discovery. She knew she was experiencing invisible loss and needed support, yet she didn't feel right talking with her friends about it. She was feeling skeptical and insecure in her marriage and found herself becoming moody and depressed.

She began to read and learned that a griever might be so invested in surviving the moment that the future seems impossible. She read that it can be frightening for a person who has suffered a loss to think ahead to the next year or month or week. She related to the newly-understood symptoms of hesitancy and withdrawal.

Nicole discovered that when a person no longer recognizes themselves, feelings like inadequacy, pointlessness, and unworthiness can surface. The grieving individual may completely lose their purpose for living. They can feel guilty for being so low and for feeling that they are bringing others down. Nicole realized that all of her feelings were normal. She learned that it is not unusual for strong, confident people to lose their self-confidence after loss, and suddenly feel weak, incapable, and insecure.

She did not want to live in survival mode and fall victim to the compounding effects of suppressing her grief. She wanted healing for herself and her husband, and their marriage. Nicole knew that he was willing and that with God, all things are possible. She had seen God completely heal her father after he had been hospitalized with a heart attack. She was confident He could heal their marriage, too.

Nicole decided to forgive her husband. The Lord led Nicole to the stronghold breaking prayers in the back of *The Breaking Negative Patterns Series* books. She helped her husband break the strongholds of Independence and Divorce, Addiction, Deception, Guilt and Shame, and Impurity.

Next, Nicole's husband helped her break the strongholds of Betrayal, Bitterness, Fear, Injustice, Loss, Prolonged Grief, and Rejection. (See many of these strongholds starting in chapter forty-four.) They also utilized the concept of the *Mental Rolodex*.

The *Mental Rolodex* technique is a short process where you allow unholy images to come up in the mind and push each one to God's throne. This practice removes the power that negative thoughts have to flash back on their own, and brings immediate supernatural healing, especially in the area of impurity and addiction.

In the workbook that correlates with this book (in the chapter *All Things are Possible with God*) you'll find the healing technique with the steps necessary for successfully deleting mental images forever.

Nicole's husband was able to find complete healing from intruding mental thoughts using this method. I learned this powerful strategy from John Alley, my pastor while I was living in Australia.

In the weeks following the stronghold breaking and *Mental Rolodex* technique, Nicole's husband did not have any questionable images come to his mind. He did one day, however, identify a dart from the enemy as he was driving around town.

He had committed to sharing everything with his wife, so he found the courage to tell Nicole that he had noticed an attractive woman and had experienced a lustful thought. He had taken the thought captive by saying, *"I take authority over lust, and I bind you in Jesus' name"* and had rejected it immediately, preventing its grip on him.

Nicole felt a difference as well. She felt God's peace and His Presence. Together, she and her husband put in place some boundaries to support his recovery and protect him from the enemy's temptation.

Some of those boundaries included him sharing the darts of the enemy against his mind, going to bed at the same time, eliminating all social media interaction with single women, eliminating online time apart, and only deleting computer history while he was with her.

They began to read Gary Chapman's book *When Sorry Isn't Enough.* Because of her husband's willingness to change and her ability to forgive, they were able to save their marriage. He is not hiding in shame and guilt, and she is no longer suffering the trauma of neglect. He now helps lead a men's group, teaching the concept of "purity in an impure world." Together with God's grace, they are better than ever.

Grief...It's Complicated

12

Compounded Grief
The Silent Avalanche

The heart was not made to grieve. Think about it. In the garden, we were meant to live *whole.*

The result of loss is the emotion *grief.* Grief is the word we use for the accumulation of feelings in response to loss. It is also the word we use for their expression through emotion. With compounded grief, the negative effects are combined, intensified, and magnified. This stress affects us spiritually, emotionally, relationally, and physically.

Often we are blinded to the symptoms and effects of grief. We don't consider that the losses we have sustained are worthy of grieving. When we don't acknowledge our losses, unprocessed feelings stay inside the heart and weigh it down. The heart can become stressed and heavy with a mentally oppressive feeling. This is where the term *heaviness* comes from.

By not addressing the heart's feelings, they are not

likely to be expressed. They are *suppressed*, which can become *compounded* during the next crisis and the next crisis, and the next crisis. Grief can slowly become an intense, psychological strain on the mind and the body.

Did you know that compounded grief can become stored in the cells of the body? Physical symptoms may begin to surface such as insomnia, hair loss, neck rigidity, body weakness, chest, and muscle pain. Grievers have reported that it affects their lungs and makes them feel like they can't get enough oxygen.

<u>If grief has compounded and has not processed, extreme stress or profound loss can trigger a person into processing all of their stored losses at once</u>. Although this event can occur throughout any time in one's life, when it happens between the approximate ages of forty and sixty, this break is usually referred to as a *mid-life crisis*.

It is critical that we acknowledge our individual losses and give our heart the time and attention that it needs and deserves to process grief. Simply acknowledging the *depth* of a loss can give the heart permission to begin to heal.

Why do we avoid grieving? The truth is, our hearts don't know *how* to grieve. The heart was not designed to grieve. Looking back to the garden, life was meant to be perfect. There was never meant to be any darkness, any loss, or any pain. The heart was not made to grieve; thus it does not know what to do with it. It does not know *how to grieve*. Additionally, we avoid it because the unknown can be scary, and it is *hard work*. We may not *want* to persevere through sadness and emotional pain. We know it takes time and it hurts so much.

13

Suppressions of Grief
The Don't Cry Lie

Suppression of feelings can be learned during childhood as we hear responses such as "Be strong" or "Don't cry" after experiencing an emotionally painful event. Sadly these phrases halt the basics of human nature; they stop the body's natural release of feelings through the expression of emotion.

Have you heard the phrase "numb the pain?" What this refers to, is the avoidance of facing the heart's true feelings. Have you heard the phrase "fill the void?" Filling the void is when a person looks for anything they can find to fill the hole in their heart; anything to occupy their mind instead of acknowledging their losses and processing through the associated grief. Yes, our feelings are invisible, but that doesn't mean they don't exist, or that they shouldn't have a voice.

Suppression of feelings prolong the healing process. The truth is that tears are the fastest way to process healing. *Tears are the secret cleansing agent within the walls of the heart.*

Some people are in survival mode, living in a constant state of grief. They may be trying to move forward with a broken heart that continues to break every day. This brokenness could be attributed to ongoing deep wounding such as infidelity or a child who has turned their back on God or their family. Could you know someone who is dealing with a history of loss that was never grieved?

A broken heart can also be due to ongoing abuse or trauma. Extreme lengths of survival mode can create Post Traumatic Stress Disorder (PTSD), a serious condition requiring stronghold breaking, prayer, and inner healing. An individual with PTSD may also require soul tie breaking and deliverance which you'll read about in the chapters ahead.

Q: Could I be grieving and not even know it?

A: Absolutely. You may have experienced multiple visible or invisible losses, but not have acknowledged them, or given your heart time to process what it was feeling.

Q: What will happen if we do not acknowledge our losses and allow our heart to express its feelings after a loss?

A: They can back up and cause a dam effect, where nothing is able to process. When we experience our next loss, it can compound behind the previous.

When we don't identify and acknowledge what we are feeling, especially when it's grief, it can lead to deep guilt. Guilt complicates the situation, compounding the initial pain and burying it deeper as new crises arise. You've just discovered what lies at the root of millions of cases of depression. *Grief.*

14

Allie's Dilemma

Allie was feeling depressed and although she couldn't see it, was displaying typical symptoms of grief. She had gained twenty pounds over the course of the year and an additional ten pounds the year before, all while working from home.

Watching her trim, fit body expand and lose its shape had been extremely difficult for her. Allie had withdrawn socially, feeling a lot of shame and sadness. She was lonely and disappointed in herself.

Often, she would find herself crying and easily overwhelmed with daily tasks, barely getting dressed for the day or combing her hair. Her husband would remind her to shower, as she had lost all interest in caring for herself.

She began to experience strange health issues including ridges in her nails, itchy rashes, and low immunity. Allie wasn't able to sleep well at night, exaggerating her foggy thinking and poor memory. Nothing really excited her anymore.

She became moody and depressed and began to experience guilt and anxiety. She spent most of her time working in front of her computer. Her husband would cook for them and bring her food. Some of her favorite times were at night when he would ask her if she wanted ice cream while they were sitting on the couch watching reality shows together.

What Allie didn't realize was that all this time she had been grieving the invisible loss of *self.* Allie was missing her well-trained physique and dogged determination. She had always been active and a healthy eater until she began to work from home.

Invisible loss can be almost impossible to identify, which is why it often becomes buried. Depression can easily be entered into as a result. To make matters worse, holding grief inside reinforces it, and Allie had been ashamed to share her feelings.

As the weight had steadily increased, so had the disappointment in herself. Allie hadn't realized that the strange feelings were connected to the grief of her weight and the loss of her drivenness.

Hiding her grief had strengthened its power and cemented it in place. It had created the effect of a hollow feeling that was searching on its own to be filled.

When we keep our feelings inside and do not allow them to come out (through emotion), our bodies begin to give us signs that it is overloaded. "Symptoms" such as headaches, ulcers, and intestinal issues can be the body's physical way of communicating its need.

As the months went on, she began to experience physical pressure on her chest and labored breathing. She had no appetite, low energy, and difficulty making simple decisions. Her husband knew that something was wrong, but could not figure it out.

Her difficulty with mental tasks and concentration was baffling. What was really concerning was her lack of attention to him and their children. She was intelligent and had often given selflessly. Her husband didn't understand the unusual impairment with daily activities or the delayed mental responses she would give.

The symptoms Allie was displaying were correlating precisely with the typical feelings that accompany grief. Often, people who are in deep sorrow are not able to take care of their own needs or the needs of those around them. This behavior is physiological and not imaginary. It's hard to take care of ourselves or those around us while we are processing loss, and Allie was experiencing a state of prolonged grief.

As soon as Allie realized she was grieving the loss of a part of herself, she decided to take action and make changes. At her husband's encouragement, they had her blood tests done. The results shouldn't have been surprising, but they were. Her thyroid wasn't working. This explained the rapid heart rate, the exertion, the low blood pressure, and the weight gain. Her lethargy and loss of motivation were making sense.

Allie's doctor prescribed her a natural thyroid medication and a natural progesterone supplement that made her feel angry. She did her best to complete her first three-month prescription but was experiencing extreme guilt caused by driving her family away. She knew she had to stop.

In nothing short of a miracle, six months later Allie received a package on her doorstep that she did not order. In it was a thyroid supplement. (The name of it is in the miscellaneous information section in the back.) She read the positive reviews online. Confused to the origin of the sender, she prayed and felt peaceful about trying it. She started on a regimen of one capsule per day, and was shocked at how good she began to feel.

Her energy was back, and the ridges in her nails were disappearing. Her moods were mellowing out, and she felt calm for the first time in a long time. She began to sleep better and the weight started to fall off.

Little by little, Allie came out of the prolonged grief. She regained her health and joy. Her marriage improved, and so did her outlook. Her confidence returned along with her zest for life. She began to plan outings and exercise and was grateful that her desire to pursue relationships had come back in full force.

15

Grief
The Needle in the Haystack

"He that is our God is the God of salvation; and unto God the Lord belong the issues from death." (Psalm 68:20)

Feelings vs. Emotion

Feelings are the *inward* personal associations in the hidden part of the heart that are acquired through experience. Although feelings are invisible, fleeting, and confusing, they want more than anything to be acknowledged.

Feelings associated with grief include:

Insecurity	Disappointment	Shame
Hopelessness	Exhaustion	Agitation
Discouragement	Lost Hope	Guilt
Depression	Weariness	Fatigue
Rejection	Deep Loss	Injustice

Anxiety	Heaviness (of the heart)
Loneliness	Feelings of Being Overwhelmed
Regret	Weakness in Resisting Opposition
Sadness	Failure and Feeling like a Failure
Frustration	Lack of Progress
Confusion	Fear of Loss
Hurt	Pain

Feelings happen *inside the heart*. They cannot be measured and are shaped by individual temperaments and impacted by past experiences. They vary from person to person, situation to situation, and experience to experience. *Feelings initiate emotion.*

Emotion is the *outward expression* of the heart's feelings. Feelings can initiate emotion such as moodiness, negative talk, anger, angry outbursts, and impulsive decisions.

A grieving person may not be able to think clearly, plan, give, or serve. It is well known that the brain does not function at full capacity when an individual is grieving (kind of like my driving mistake after our house burned down in chapter six). Often the person becomes indifferent and loses interest in discussions and things happening around them.

Indecision and confusion are common in grief and grievers can feel like they're stuck. Physical symptoms of loss often include insomnia, inverted sleep patterns, changes in energy levels or appetite, and weight gain.

16

Seven Signs of Hidden Grief

Mourning means "signs of sorrow" and happens in the heart. Interestingly, the Bible states that those who have pride struggle to mourn. *"And ye are puffed up, and have not rather mourned."* (1 Corinthians 5:2)

Below is the definition of the word *mourn*:

verb (used *without* object)

1. to feel or express sorrow or grief.
2. to grieve or lament for the dead.
3. to show the conventional or usual signs of sorrow over a person's death.

verb (used with object)

4. to feel or express sorrow or grief over a misfortune, loss, or anything regretted.
5. to grieve or lament over (someone who has died).
6. to utter in a sorrowful manner (sound).

Uncovering Hidden Grief

Grieving individuals may find themselves emotional, distracted, and tearing up frequently. Loss is an event, and grief is the subsequent experience that stirs up feelings, which in turn produce emotion. The value that was placed upon the object of affection will determine the depth of a loss.

The following symptoms can help identify hidden grief:

Consistent Infirmity	Pressure
Withdrawal	Self-Absorption
Abuse of Self	Foggy Thinking
Relationship Difficulty	Escaping Reality
Isolation	Negative Coping Behaviors
Negativity	Denial
Giving Up or Giving In	Loss
Discouragement	Complaining

<u>Below are seven signs of hidden grief:</u>

1. Loss of feeling safe. Crises can cause one to wonder whether their world is safe anymore. Prior assumptions may be shattered. Unreasonable or uncontrollable fear may hit, and anxiety or panic attacks can surface.

2. Loss of ability to focus. The mind can seem desensitized to everything but the crisis. Symptoms can affect the *brain,* including impairment of mental tasks including difficulty concentrating, poor memory, anxiety with decision making, and delayed responses. Those grieving might forget how to drive to familiar places or follow basic routines.

3. Loss of motivation. Other aspects of life might seem insignificant. Much may need to be accomplished, but fogginess and confusion can make a person skeptical of making decisions. Grievers often fall into depression, as they fall behind on priorities that begin to pile up; there can be a sense of being out of control. This feeling can create a sense of futility and helplessness.

4. Loss of inner joy. Things that once gave pleasure may seem gone. When a person is in pain, and when they are grieving, JOY can become a non-existent word that can be hard to relate to. This is normal. It can take a long time to even *think* of happiness, let alone joy, again.

5. Loss of spirituality or feeling close to God. During grief, belief systems can suddenly be turned inside out and upside down. Grievers may struggle with spiritual questions after a loss, initiating a *faith crisis.* These spiritual crises can often lead to disorienting questions about faith and feelings of doubt and guilt. Confusion can settle in when the process is not understood. Those suffering profound loss can find themselves directing anger toward God and thus seeming to sever a once close relationship. Some never come out of their faith crisis, whereas others come out with their faith stronger.

6. Loss of ability to make decisions. Indecision is common after loss. Decisions take concentration, and grievers often find it difficult to focus enough to see choices. Even simple things like choosing what to eat for dinner or what clothes to wear may feel overwhelming. Because of the insecurity and lack of self-trust, they can find themselves wondering *What should I do?* in the simplest of decisions.

7. Loss of desire to maintain friendships. Grievers isolate. Their energy is sapped. They may find that they have no effort or care to give. They may feel guilty that they are not helping others or carrying their load in a relationship. They might wonder what is wrong with themselves and others might wonder, too.

If there are losses that have been sustained but not processed, extreme stress or loss, like the loss of a family member, can trigger the body and heart into processing all of the consolidated losses at once. Identifying and grieving unprocessed losses, one at a time, is much more proactive and healthy than bearing consolidated grief.

17

What do Grief Counselors Advise?

"God is our refuge and strength, a very present help in trouble." (Psalm 46:1)

After researching ideas from grief counselors, it's clear that most grievers really want to feel better.

<u>The following is a consolidated list (in no particular order) of twenty-one practical things you can do to begin to process your grief and help yourself cope.</u>

1. Try to spend as much time alone with God as possible. "The LORD bindeth up the breach of his people, and healeth the stroke of their wound." (Isaiah 30:26)

2. It will help to surround yourself with people who will support and comfort you. People who are loyal, helpful, caring, and kind will allow you time to grieve. Pull close to the people you know who have empathy, emotional stability, compassion, a serving mentality, warmth, patience, tolerance, and who understand your slow pace. In the book *Safe People,* the authors discuss how people often think of the apostle Paul as a 'spiritual giant' who was somehow so spiritual that he didn't need anything from others. "Paul writes that the encouragement and love of others kept him going through all of his difficult times. We must remember that we are never so 'spiritual' that we do not need the encouragement that God provides through other people." [2]

3. Try to avoid stressful situations. It's better to be alone and at peace than to be around drama and have anxiety.

4. Sit in the sun for fifteen minutes per day. The vitamin D our skin produces from the sun improves our outlook, and is necessary for many of the body's functions.

5. If you have the energy, find a way to volunteer or help other people in need. Serving others is like medicine to the soul.

6. Refuse to listen to negative dream killers. They will pull you down and discourage you.

7. Try to be content and limit complaining.

8. Bring plants indoors. The inside of your house may need to become different, although you'll want to maintain familiarity in the home environment.

9. Look to someone who has prayed for you or given you wise counsel in the past. You may feel guilty sharing feelings and emotions with a person is also grieving. If they are not comfortable hearing you discuss your pain, find an individual who is neutral with

---

[2] Cloud H. & Townsend, J., *Safe People* (Zondervan, 2016).

whom to share your feelings. Getting their perspective, at a time like this, is invaluable.

10. Connect with people who display enthusiasm and spontaneity.

11. Take naps if your body needs them. Grievers often experience sleep inversion where they are awake at opposite times of their typical schedule. Give your body the grace it needs during this difficult time.

12. Read some of your past journal entries. See where God has brought you. Did you know that journaling on paper a minimum of three times per week has been known to reduce worry, anxiety, insomnia, and stress? There are many studies available on the benefits of journaling.

13. Beware of the natural tendency to overindulge in food while grieving. It's easy to use food for comfort, but the extra calories will pack on weight and cause compounded grief on a whole new level.

14. Do not make significant changes or life-changing decisions while you're grieving.

15. Make phone calls to some friends you haven't talked to in a while. Tell them you've been thinking about them and ask how you can pray for them.

16. Don't allow yourself to become depressed. Moving through the stages of grief can be complicated, as they are interchangeable and there is no timetable. It is well known that the amount of time grief takes to work itself through is far longer than is expected. Some people function in a continual state of grief throughout their life, which is not necessary. If you lost a loved one, the person you lost would want you to be happy and go on, living life to its fullest. The fourth edition of the Diagnostic and Statistical Manual of Mental Disorders (DSM-IV), from the American Psychiatric Association, set the average time for grieving at two months. The newer, DSM-V published in 2013, changed this period to one to two years. Additionally, after the loss of a *loved one,* we are defined as newly bereaved for at least the first full five years.

17. Don't isolate yourself. Proverbs 27:9 says, *"Ointment and perfume rejoice the heart: so doth the sweetness of a man's friend by hearty counsel."* Share what's going on with a burden bearer or intercessor. They'll support you spiritually and lift you up in prayer during troubling times. Share your feelings and ask for prayer and insight. These individuals will be a precious source of comfort, as they sit quietly with you while you grieve. Their love, kindness, tenderness, and caring will give you the strength to go on. If you don't have anyone to pray for you, search online for the closest Healing Rooms, where there's always prayer support.

18. Return to your hobbies. Get back to what brings you joy.

19. Don't let grief define you. Create a new normal.

20. Try to keep your head up while you wait patiently for the grief to pass.

21. Smile! Even if you don't feel like it. It's psychological, and it really helps!

Soul Ties

18

Unspoken Connections

"Behold, how good and how pleasant it is for brethren to dwell together in unity! It is like the precious ointment upon the head, that ran down upon the beard, even Aaron's beard: that went down to the skirts of his garments." (Psalm 133:1-3)

God designed us to live in unity and He calls us to love deeply. He created our hearts to trust, hope, and give. The definition of a *soul tie* is to *bond together*. It's like an unspoken connection. It means to knit two souls in mind, will, and emotion. The word *knit* means to join together or to bind up. Ecclesiastes 4:12 states, *"And if one prevail against him, two shall withstand him; and a threefold cord is not quickly broken."*

Soul ties were designed by God to be a blessing to our lives. I Samuel 18:1 tells us that Jonathan's soul was *knit* to the soul of David. *"And it came to pass when he had made an end of speaking unto Saul, that the soul of Jonathan was knit with the soul of David, and Jonathan loved him as his own soul."*

Positive emotional ties exist in balanced, functional relationships such as healthy parent-child dynamics, deep friendships, and close loving marriages. These emotional connections are meant to be a blessing from the Lord as they bond relationships, create strength, and unite us.

We are reminded in scripture to be wise in our relationships. *"Be not deceived: evil communications corrupt good manners."* (1 Corinthians 15:33) We are told to avoid close associations with those who are angry, act foolishly, or are unbelievers. The Bible calls it a *snare to the soul.* Proverbs 22:24-25 states, *"Make no friendship with an angry man; and with a furious man thou shalt not go: Lest thou learn his ways, and get a snare to thy soul."*

I always picture soul ties like a fishing line with hooks in it, connecting two people's hearts. This is fine in healthy relationships. Unfortunately, because of our fallen world, relationships can turn sour, and soul ties can become distorted. The problem arises when a relationship is toxic or controlling, or the relationship continues to be a source of continual stress or grief for us after it is over. These heart covenants can keep individuals bound in negative ways. Next, we will learn about Natasha's soul tie and how to identify and break one.

19

Natasha's Soul Tie

Natasha attended a large high school in Ohio with over four thousand students. During her sophomore year, she met Daniel, a track and field athlete who excelled at everything he did. He soon captured her heart. Natasha and Daniel spent much time together on the phone sharing the details of their days, and their feelings seemed to grow for each other.

Daniel was attracted to the international girls on campus. He was popular, and over the next two years, she found herself afraid of being honest about her feelings. Although Natasha was secretly jealous of the time he spent with other girls, she didn't want to appear needy and didn't want him to know how much she really cared. Deep in her heart, she always believed Daniel would prioritize her. The longer they were friends, the more of herself she gave.

Daniel graduated the year before Natasha, and moved several hours away to attend trade school. Although she missed him terribly, her senior year flew by. When school ended, Natasha moved out of state to attend college. She found herself loving life and eventually lost contact with him.

After college, Natasha went home and reached out to Daniel. They hadn't spoken in almost two years and as she heard him say that he had recently gotten married, her heart sank. She was devastated with the heartbreaking news.

Even though they had lived separate lives and she had never shared her feelings, Natasha knew deep inside, that her heart had always belonged to him. She silently grieved the invisible loss. With broken dreams ahead of her, she wondered if she'd be able to love again.

Her heart healed slowly. Three years later, Natasha found a new love, who later became her husband. After a quick engagement, they were married in an exotic park under the blossoming cherry trees, a desire that had been dreamed up by her and Daniel years before.

A few months into her marriage, Natasha realized how much she missed Daniel. Memories often came to her mind as she wondered about him. *Where was he? Was he happy? Why hadn't she shared her true feelings? Was he her true soul mate?*

Her private thoughts haunted her. She felt guilty and tried not to compare her marriage with the illusion of what could have been with Daniel. When she argued with her husband, she found herself retreating and wishfully thinking about a life with Daniel. Her fantasizing was becoming an almost daily occurrence, and she knew it was starting to have the potential to damage her marriage.

20

When the Heart Won't Let Go

One night at home group, Natasha learned about soul ties. She learned that there can be an unspoken connection that remains after a relationship ends. She knew that her heart was still very much connected to Daniel and she also recognized on a fundamental level that it was wrong.

There was no doubt that they still had a soul tie. Now that she had committed her life to Christ and to her husband, she wanted her heart only connected to his. Natasha could feel the Holy Spirit's conviction and knew that God was stepping in to protect her marriage and keep it sacred. He was definitely speaking to her. Natasha decided to schedule a meeting with her pastor's wife.

She was nervous about sharing, but knew she needed to be honest about her feelings. During the meeting, the pastor's wife confirmed that Natasha most likely did have a soul tie, and within just a few minutes, she helped Natasha break it. There was instant release! The internal stress was gone. Natasha felt a freedom that she hadn't felt for a long time. In the weeks following, she didn't think about Daniel once, or dream about him, either. She finally was able to move forward.

Breaking soul ties is a tool for setting the heart free. In the chapters ahead, you'll find strategies and tools that have been successful in helping many find healing. You'll learn more about soul ties and will be given a step-by-step strategy to help yourself and others get set free.

Soul ties can be exchanged through a variety of encounters including an idolatrous relationship, a dysfunctional and emotional involvement, or a sexual encounter. Because of the dysfunction, a high percentage of these relationships do not last long term, and when they end there can be a fracturing loss evolving from the severing of the relationship.

The remaining unspoken connections can be the cause of much grief. Cutting these ties can be refreshing, healing, and freeing. This is called *Soul Tie Breaking*.

<u>The most common soul ties come out of the following twenty-one types of relationships:</u>

1. Past exes.

2. Past loves.

3. Past intimate encounters.

4. A relationship with someone who has passed away.

5. An important relationship that was ripped apart by a move, family, friends, fate, job transfers, etc.

6. A relationship that has ended that is difficult to let go, where thoughts about the other person are continual.

7. Any manipulative relationships which cause guilt and grief.

8. Idolatrous relationships where one or both parties are on a pedestal.

9. Current or past relationships where one person is used or controlled.

10. Dysfunctional relationships where one person severely depends on the other emotionally.

11. Relationships in which there is mental, verbal, emotional, psychological, spiritual, or physical abuse.

12. Past friendships or business relationships that abused trust including betrayal, accusation, backstabbing, theft, or deception.

13. Parent/child or husband/wife relationships where there is neglect including a lack of love, safety, or comfort. Love, safety, and comfort naturally fill the soul, and the neglect of any one of these will wound and create trauma; it can open a gap or a leave a void in the soul.

14. Leadership that has had an extended, disturbing level of control over one's life.

15. Current or past involvement with any organization or religion which impresses a controlling culture upon the attendees or propagates false teachings. (This includes organizations where vows must be spoken, severely strict churches which abuse spiritually, cults, and orders like Freemasonry.)

16. Relationships that lack privacy, respect, or boundaries. For example, a partner secretly going through the other's belongings or phone or listening in on their private conversations.

17. Parent/child dynamics where the child controls the parents with demands and selfishness.

18. Dysfunction in the parent relationship as they try to manipulate and control the child after they are an adult, using them, and making them feel obligated through guilt. Phrases often used include "I *need* you to do me a favor," "I'm disappointed with you," or "After all your father and I have done for you."

19. Family pets that are no longer with the family.

20. Any heart covenant made with a person who is gone.

21. An acquaintance who keeps coming to mind over and over.

If you have identified that you need to break soul ties, there is hope! You'll want to pray *The Soul Tie Breaking Prayer* in chapter thirty-nine. Chapter thirty-two will provide directions on *Soul Tie Breaking.* There you will be given the tools and we will walk through each step together.

21

Soul Tie Q & A

"Stand fast therefore in the liberty wherewith Christ hath made us free, and be not entangled again with the yoke of bondage." (Galatians 5:1)

Q: What clues I can look for to identify a soul tie?

A: Any one of these four signs can indicate a soul tie:

1. A continual pull on the heart toward a person, especially in the context of toxic relationships.

2. Relationships with an active element of control, which are usually built and maintained through guilt, fear, deception, and manipulation.

3. Ruminations (continual negative thoughts, memories, or replaying of interactions) that repeat over and over involving a specific person.

4. A strong sense of obligation to a person who has extremely high expectations.

Q: Are there any differences in soul ties when you compare a breakup and a death?

A: No, other than a person who is alive can continue living without you. A breakup involves one or both parties making a conscious choice to end a relationship, which involves the other person continuing to grow, thrive, and exist without you. Them choosing to continue living their life *apart* can contribute to additional pain.

Q: I still think about my ex, and I'm pretty sure I have a soul tie. What should I do?

A: There's a reason the person is an ex. Relationships are complicated in nature, and there can be deep pain in breakups such as betrayal, disappointment, heartbreak, and even revenge. If intimacy was involved, it can be even more devastating. God designed sex and love to be an amazing and powerful combination. When sex and love don't end in a lifetime of marriage, the result can be severe heartbreak and a soul tie. (See chapter thirty-nine for a specific soul-tie prayer for this situation.)

Q: Can someone have a soul tie with their pet?

A: The term soul tie implies the bondings of the soul. A being that has a soul in it can think, have feelings, and show emotion; this can include animals, who have a soul in the respect that they can think, express feelings, and have memories just as humans do. If you have had an animal, you have probably experienced a bond with a pet and know that they can very much be a member of the family. If you or someone you know (even a child) have a lost a pet and still feel a hole in the heart, see chapter thirty-nine for a specific prayer to break that soul tie.

Q: I broke a soul tie with someone who is no longer in my life, but I'm often reminded of them when I see an object that we shared or something that they gave me. Is the object creating a soul tie again?

A: Usually, when we enter into a new season, there is a correlating physical purging that happens to some degree. If there are objects in your living space that are keeping you connected to a person whom you've released through soul tie breaking, you may prayerfully want to consider letting the objects go; this might include destroying them, selling them, or giving them away. Ask the Lord to show you what to do with them.

Q: I'm in a rocky relationship with someone whom I cannot break contact with. There have been some issues in the past that have hurt us both. Can I cut a soul tie and continue in a relationship with them?

A: The short answer is yes. Did you know that it is possible to *cleanse* the connection you have with someone? If things have turned sour, you can pray and ask the Lord to cleanse the connection between you. I like to visualize the Lord taking a scrub brush and cleaning the cord (picture a fishing line) that connects the two hearts and removing any dark debris that was part of it. I see it sparkling white when He's done. I ask Him to remove what was bad and preserve what is good. I can always feel an immediate difference in the spirit realm and in my connection with the person after I pray the cleansing prayer ahead.

Q: I lost a loved one quite a while ago, and I'm still struggling. Could I have a soul tie with them even though they have passed away?

A: Yes, you can. There is a prayer in chapter thirty-nine that will guide you in thanking God for the blessing that they were to your life. It will lead you in cleansing your memories and releasing your loved one.

Q: I broke a soul tie with someone who I am still friends with on social media. I never have a good feeling when I think of them. What should I do?

A: If you broke a soul tie with a person, there was a reason. Keeping them as a friend on social media is keeping the door open to interaction with them, their opinions, and their drama. More importantly, it's inviting the potential for a future relationship. Is that what you secretly want? If not, make a decision to close the door on the negativity they bring. Have the courage to put a stop to it once and for all. If it ever comes up in a future conversation, you can simply say that the connection made you feel uncomfortable. No one can argue with something that makes you feel uncomfortable.

Q: I have a very strong ungodly soul tie with someone, but I'm scared to break it. Why do I feel this way?

A: If the thought of breaking an ungodly soul tie seems devastating, there's a good chance that a stronghold of Idolatry is holding the bond in place. Idolatry puts a thing or a person up on a pedestal; it makes things glitter and distorts the reality of the relationship. In situations like this, it is recommended that the stronghold of Idolatry be broken. Directions on breaking this stronghold can be found in chapter forty-eight. It's important that you free yourself by breaking the soul tie and stronghold simultaneously.

Burden Bearing

22

The Five Gallon Bucket Person

"Bear ye one another's burdens, and so fulfill the law of Christ." (Galatians 6:2)

Cindy is out camping with her family. They are sitting around the campfire, and the sun is setting. She is having a perfect evening with her children and her husband. They don't get to enjoy nights like this often. The only issue is the mosquitoes that are landing on her kids.

She gets up to apply her essential oils around the campsite to be sure she can protect her family. She then overhears the neighbors having the same problem. She knows that mosquitoes can carry malaria and dangerous viruses which can sabotage the autoimmune system. She leaves her campsite to help the neighbors.

When she finishes, she continues to the next site to help another family. She seems to be the only one who thought to bring her bug repelling oils. Even though her family is waiting, she knows she can protect the campers from being bitten by mosquitoes.

Cindy is a "burden bearer" as well as what I like to call a *Five Gallon Bucket* person. She has a lot of love to give, compared to a one-gallon or a one-cup person and is willing to put the needs of others before her own. While not all of us are natural Five Gallon Bucket people, we can certainly aspire to become one.

<u>Burden bearers have genuine hearts that feel deeply for others. They take the following scriptures very seriously.</u>

1. "This is my commandment, That ye love one another, as I have loved you. Greater love hath no man than this, that a man lay down his life for his friends." (John 15:12-13)

2. "Rejoice with them that do rejoice, and weep with them that weep." (Romans 12:15)

3. "And whether one member suffers, all the members suffer with it; or one member be honoured, all the members rejoice with it." (1 Corinthians 12:26)

4. "Present your bodies a living sacrifice, holy, acceptable unto God, which is your reasonable service." (Romans 12:1)

In the chapters ahead, you'll learn how to recognize burden bearers. You'll also discover points of caution to keep burden bearing from becoming a *personal* burden.

23

Understand It

Burden bearing is the first calling, and primary labor of every Christian and some are called specifically, to be *burden bearers*. Burden bearing, I believe, is the gift of compassion combined with a prophetic gift. It is commonly displayed through intercession (prayer), and is often expressed as love in action, or *acts of service*.

Burden bearers offer their bodies as "living sacrifices." They feel the hurt that others experience and vividly *see* the problems of others. They are strongly compelled to act, often helping with creative solutions. They are used by the Lord to lighten the load and share information with others. They come alongside and hold up the arms of those who are wearied and battle fatigued, in the midst of their trials and temptations.

In the Bible, Moses' brother Aaron is an excellent example of a burden bearer. Aaron spoke for Moses when he couldn't speak himself and also physically held his arms up at a crucial point during an Israelite battle.

Jesus is our example of the ultimate burden bearer. Isaiah 53:4 tells us, *"Surely he hath borne our griefs, and carried our sorrows: yet we did esteem him stricken, smitten of God, and afflicted."* He took on the sin of the world and intercedes for us.

Many burden bearers have experienced trauma in their lives. They might also have a collection of wounds that have built up in their heart over the years. Their memories may be more painful than others are willing to acknowledge.

Prone to carrying guilt and shame, trauma (witnessed, experienced, or perceived) affects them deeply, and they may struggle for years to heal wounds on their own.

Burden bearers easily sense what others feel and are unusually empathetic. They readily *absorb* the emotion of those around them; because of this, they tend to grieve over their own losses, as well as the losses of others.

Burden bearing might sometimes feel like a curse. One may miss out on enjoying life with those they love because they are helping others. In Cindy's camping story, she returned from helping the neighbors to find that the campfire was out and the kids were tucked in their sleeping bags. Along with her family, she was disappointed that she missed out on a special time to make memories.

Burden bearing is the heart of God being expressed in human form. It's the purest expression of love there is; *to lay down our life for another*. Ahead you'll find some points of caution that burden bearers and those who love them should be aware of.

24

Points of Caution

"See then that ye walk circumspectly, not as fools, but as wise." (Ephesians 5:15)

From my observations, burden bearers often display physical symptoms in their bodies. These may include stomach or joint pains, unusual discomfort, depressive episodes, and other unexplained moods.

You can see in Lamentations 2:11 the burden bearer who is deeply grieving over the destruction of others as if it were their own. Read the severe effect it is having on their body. *"Mine eyes do fail with tears, my bowels are troubled, my liver is poured upon the earth, for the destruction of the daughter of my people; because the children and the sucklings swoon in the streets of the city."*

We know that emotion can be stored in the body. Grief, in particular, can affect the lungs. It can make breathing difficult and can make a person feel like they aren't getting enough oxygen. These symptoms may be a signal for burden bearers to pray for someone.

Unfortunately, most burden bearers think there is something wrong with themselves, and they spend unnecessary time and money searching for cures. Burden bearing can sometimes be painful as we tangibly carry the physical pain of another as our own. Acknowledging that the discomfort may be the effect of bearing the burden for someone else is a huge milestone.

If it happens to be someone else's burden, the best thing the burden bearer can do for relief is to release the issue to God through prayer and wait, before scheduling multiple medical tests or taking unnecessary trips to the doctor. Praying in one's heavenly language makes this task simple.

<u>The following list provides ten points of caution that burden bearers and those who love them should be aware of and provide grace for:</u>

1. Burden bearers can burn out under the weight of everyone's troubles. They engage heavily, quickly committing to carrying the burdens of others and bearing them as their own.

2. Burden bearers can have such compassion for others that they put themselves at risk. They also struggle with setting boundaries in place. They often struggle to say *"no"* when others ask for favors. They do not want to hurt anyone's feelings or come across as uncaring; this can be especially detrimental when it comes to *finances*. They can be gullible and easily talked into things. They may want to help even when they don't have resources. They might overextend themselves to help irresponsible people, bringing worry and unnecessary problems into their world as they carry the financial burdens of others.

3. Burden bearers generally grieve very deeply. They may at times feel stuck in life as they process lengthy periods of loss. This prolonged grief can often be misinterpreted as depression or a mood disorder. They can also tend to be susceptible to carrying compounded grief because they neglect to push burdens up to God.

4. Burden bearers are sensitive to the atmosphere. They are highly sensitive in ways that those around may not understand. They can be sensitive to places and environments as well as negative media, movies, and the world's culture in today's society. They sense the defilement in the world, and this defilement can bring about a *heaviness*. They may come across as pensive and uncomfortable at times as they try to process what they are feeling and why.

5. Often burden bearers are physically sensitive. They often observe changes in their body, their mind, or their habits and worry about their health. Another scripture in Lamentations 1:20 says, *"Behold, O Lord; for I am in distress: my bowels are troubled; mine heart is turned within me."*

6. Most burden bearers have a prophetic gift, and they must guard against its perversion. They must take caution not to assume what others are thinking and to stay free from deception, idolatry, and judgment.

7. Burden bearers can tend to become fearful and worry about things, which can open the door to doubt. They carry the weight of it all, which leads to anxiety, instead of interceding and asking the Lord to take the burden of the world from off of their shoulders.

They need to pray for faith (the opposite of fear) and give problems to God.

8. Burden bearers can be tempted into the idolatry of "self." They may not trust the Lord to intervene and help carry problems. This distrust can lead to spiritual pride and the belief that *I have to bear this because no one else is able.*

9. Burden bearers can tend to live a quiet, lonely existence if not intentional about getting out. They are best paired with friends and family who relentlessly encourage them to have fun.

10. Burden bearers are prone to absorbing the projections of other people. They are unique and may be referred to as the "cry baby" or the family's *sensitive* one. The truth is, they are *vulnerable* to the looks, words, moods, and emotions of others. They may struggle to separate their feelings and needs from those of others. Without the Holy Spirit's guidance and understanding, they can tend to find themselves isolated, depressed, confused, and disillusioned. I have a friend whose fifteen-month-old son cries whenever another person cries. She calls him her *sympathy crier.* He is a beautiful example of an individual who was given this gift at conception. We have a loving God who has created each of us with unique giftings to encourage and support each other and to bear one another's burdens, so fulfilling the law of Christ. *"Bear ye one another's burdens, and so fulfil the law of Christ."* (Galatians 6:2)

25

Obedience is Better than Sacrifice

"And Samuel said, Hath the Lord as great delight in burnt offerings and sacrifices, as in obeying the voice of the Lord? Behold, to obey is better than sacrifice, and to hearken than the fat of rams." (1 Samuel 15:22)

Burden bearers must guard against serving, just to *serve. Good opportunities can become distractions if God is not calling us to them.* If you are obligated to activities or people whom God has not called you to, you may be burning yourself out and more importantly, taking someone else's opportunity for growth.

Over the years, I've shared in many ministry and prayer experiences. Recently, God has called me to focus on writing. In my current season, I am accepting fewer ministry opportunities. *Why?* Being a burden bearer myself, my heart is continuously drawn to help others. When I go out, I often find myself staying up late to support or pray for others, which causes me to sleep in the next day. I may even have revelatory dreams that night with solutions for how to help the people who I met the night before.

Waking up later, cuts into several hours of my writing time which I plan for early each morning. You may wonder, *Couldn't you do both?* The answer is, in *this* season is no. Because I literally carry their burden, I have tried it, and I am drained; so drained, in fact, that I am not able to give my best to this writing assignment that God *is* calling me to.

> "Happy is the man who knows his limitations and refuses to accept another responsibility unless he can complete the one for which he is presently accountable. It is far better to do a good job of a few things than a poor job of many things."[3]
> -Tim LaHaye, *Spirit-Controlled Temperament*

I know I must daily choose obedience to my writing assignment. *Can I share my struggle?* It hasn't been easy! Being shut in writing for a long time has been a serious sacrifice. I miss my friends, my family, my career... my life! I very much look forward to completing this series and moving into my next assignment. The hardest part is not knowing how long it will take. Having unknowns in the future can naturally be cause for worry. I must continually lift the unknowns in my future to God.

In the *Breaking Negative Patterns Workbook,* I share some of the opposition that I've experienced during this assignment. It's so obvious, it's almost laughable. I write because the Lord has called me to it and I will always answer His call, no matter how much of a sacrifice. The Lord has laid His life down for me and I have committed to laying my life down for Him.

---

[3] LaHaye T., *Spirit-Controlled Temperament (*Tyndale House Publishers, 1994).

26

Training for the Burden Bearer

Burden bearing can be a struggle and can often be tiring, but it doesn't have to be a dark cloud. Learn to understand burden bearing by reading and praying about it.

Burden bearing is the work of the Lord. It's a part of intercession, which is a unique form of prayer. Burden bearing is accomplished through the Holy Spirit working in us and should not be done in our own power. Other forms of prayer may begin in man's heart (thanksgiving, petition), but intercession begins in the heart of God.

The most important thing to remember, is to take burdens to God's throne and pray in the spirit to release them. Become God's instrument. Allow His comfort to be expressed through you to the person for whom you intercede. Burden bearers may focus on all of the things wrong in the world, and this is where they must pray and lift everything to God. The stress and pressure become too heavy and harmful when *we* try to carry it.

Lift burdens up and move on. This must become a daily maintenance; otherwise, burden bearers can become heavy with *the cares of this world.* Lifting burdens up is as easy as seeing a picture of God's throne in heaven and seeing all of the burdens being put into a basket. I often see His hands coming down to take the basket from my hands. I always instantly feel lighter.

Burden bearing is light only when we are following the Lord's agenda. We must allow the Lord to do it *in* us, and share in what *He* is doing. Unfortunately, many live their whole life without figuring this out.

<u>The following are fourteen strategies to keep burden bearing from becoming a personal burden:</u>

1. Keep the Sabbath and rest. You desperately need it.

2. Never allow your feelings to control you.

3. Learn to distinguish your feelings and emotion from the feelings and emotion of others.

4. Use wisdom in new relationships. Burden bearers are easily drawn into dysfunctional relationships. The stakes are high that devoted burden bearers will attract manipulating narcissists. *Users love burden bearers.* They sucker them in with a false optimism and then take advantage of them, abuse them, and wreak havoc on every aspect of their existence. Burden bearers can be rescuers, peacemakers, and enablers, and they tend to blame themselves as they pick up the slack for the shortcomings of those around them. This dysfunction can create contempt and deep wounding in the individual. *In Sheep's Clothing,* is a powerful book about this by Dr. George Simon. In it he teaches how to recognize manipulation maneuvers. Read it! It may change your life! He also has videos available on YouTube.

5. Set and maintain boundaries in relationships, especially those that are dysfunctional. Burden bearers can often be taken advantage of. Sensitive-hearted, compassionate burden bearers can appear to be vulnerable prey and must be on the lookout for manipulating abusers. They don't see them coming, and end up being persuaded into doing things that they are uncomfortable with, but don't feel they can back out of. Burden bearers must use *wisdom* with their gift of compassion. *You can be a good person with a kind heart and still say "no."*

6. It's crucial that burden bearers use discretion; this is especially true when it comes to sharing the problems of others. Burden bearers can be tempted to share people's problems when they are not around. They must remember to lift their personal issues and the issues of others to God.

7. Thank God for the positives. If you can't think of any, ask a loved one to remind you. Use your journal and write down the positives in your life. Journaling them will trigger the thoughts to flow.

8. Assist others in teaching them how to lift their burdens up. "Blessed be God, even the Father of our Lord Jesus Christ, the Father of mercies, and the God of all comfort; Who comforteth us in all our tribulation, that we may be able to comfort them which are* *in any trouble, by the comfort wherewith we ourselves are comforted of God."* (2 Corinthians 1:3-4)

9. Develop hobbies and enjoy a balance of activities. Release energy and process thoughts through exercise and fun.

10. Join a prayer group in which intercession is shared.

11. Release the need to help everyone with everything.

12. Protect your heart from being discouraged or depressed. Turn a deaf ear on negative people, negative news, and negative stories.

13. Praise God. Psalm 100 tells us to *"Shout for joy to the Lord, all the earth. Worship the Lord with gladness; come before him with joyful songs."*

14. Breathe in the aroma of orange, grapefruit, or rose. These scents have been used for generations to provide relief from depressive symptoms. Essential oils can enhance your environment and can be inhaled through the use of a diffuser to provide a boost during times of stress and fatigue. Info on what Eli and I use can be found in the miscellaneous information section in the back. *"God, thy God, hath anointed thee with the oil of gladness above thy fellows. All thy garments smell of myrrh, and aloes, and cassia, out of the ivory palaces, whereby they have made thee glad."* (Psalm 45:7-8)

Preparation for Healing

27

Healing of the Heart in Hebrew Culture

"Blessed are they that mourn: for they shall be comforted." (Matthew 5:4)

The Bible is full of examples of mourning. It was an essential part of the culture of the Jews, and they intentionally factored it into their lifestyle. The ability of the culture to express their signs of sorrow helped to heal their broken hearts.

<u>Below are scriptures along with some interesting facts the Bible teaches concerning grief during Biblical times.</u>

There were certain people set apart for grieving.

Jeremiah 9:17 "Thus saith the Lord of hosts, Consider ye, and call for the mourning women, that they may come;"

Amos 5:16 "Alas! alas! and they shall call the husbandman to mourning, and such as are skillful of lamentation to wailing."

People made appointments to grieve with their friends.

Job 2:11 "Now when Job's three friends heard of all this evil that was come upon him, they came everyone from his own place; Eliphaz the Temanite, and Bildad the Shuhite, and Zophar the Naamathite: for they had made an appointment together to come to mourn with him and to comfort him."

There was a place they could go to grieve.

Ecclesiastes 7:2 "It is better to go to the house of mourning."

Jeremiah 16:5 "For thus saith the Lord, Enter not into the house of mourning..."

There were set times and seasons for grieving.

Esther 9:22 "As the days wherein the Jews rested from their enemies, and the month which was turned unto them from sorrow to joy, and from mourning into a good day: that they should make them days of feasting and joy, and of sending portions one to another, and gifts to the poor."

The word "bitter" describes losing an only child or first born.

Zechariah 12:10 "They shall mourn for him, as one mourneth for his only son, and shall be in bitterness for him, as one that is in bitterness for his firstborn."

There was collective mourning among people, which means many would grieve at the same time.

Numbers 20:29 "When all the congregation saw that Aaron was dead, they mourned for Aaron thirty days, even all the house of Israel."

Proverbs 29:2 "When the righteous are in authority, the people rejoice: but when the wicked beareth rule, the people mourn."

Joel 1:9 "The priests, the Lord's ministers, mourn."

Zechariah 12:12 "The land shall mourn, every family apart; the family of the house of David apart, and their wives apart; the family of the house of Nathan apart, and their wives apart."

Revelation 18:11 "The merchants of the earth shall weep and mourn over her; for no man buyeth their merchandise anymore."

Ecclesiastes 12:5 "Man goeth to his long home and the mourners go about the streets."

Matthew 24:30 "Then shall appear the sign of the Son of man in heaven: and then shall all the tribes of the earth mourn, and they shall see the Son of man coming in the clouds of heaven with power and great glory."

Esther 4:3 "In every province, whithersoever the king's commandment and his decree came, there was great mourning among the Jews, and fasting, and weeping, and wailing; and many lay in sackcloth and ashes."

Individuals cried in addition to mourning.

Deuteronomy 34:8 "So the days of weeping and mourning for Moses were ended."

2 Samuel 1:12 "And they mourned, and wept;"

Isaiah 22:12 "In that day did the Lord God of hosts call to weeping, and to mourning;"

Matthew 2:18 "In Rama was there a voice heard, lamentation, and weeping, and great mourning;"

Mark 16:10 "They mourned and wept."

Revelation 18:11 "The merchants of the earth shall weep and mourn over her;"

Clothing was impacted during mourning.

Genesis 37:34 "Jacob rent his clothes, and put sackcloth upon his loins, and mourned for his son;"

2 Samuel 14:2 "Joab sent to Tekoah, and fetched thence a wise woman, and said unto her, I pray thee, feign thyself to be a mourner, and put on now mourning apparel;"

Isaiah 22:12 "In that day did the Lord God of hosts call to ...girding with sackcloth:"

Jeremiah 6:26 "O daughter of my people, gird thee with sackcloth, and wallow thyself in ashes: make thee mourning, as for an only son, most bitter lamentation:"

Amos 8:10 "I will turn your feasts into mourning, and all your songs into lamentation; and I will bring up sackcloth upon all loins, and baldness upon every head; and I will make it as the mourning of an only son, and the end thereof as a bitter day."

Micah 1:8 "Therefore I will wail and howl, I will go stripped and naked: I will make a wailing like the dragons, and mourning as the owls."

There were varying amounts of times that they grieved.

Genesis 37:34 "Jacob... mourned for his son many days."

Numbers 20:29 "When all the congregation saw that Aaron was dead, they mourned for Aaron thirty days, even all the house of Israel."

Deuteronomy 34:8 "The children of Israel wept for Moses in the plains of Moab thirty days: so the days of weeping and mourning for Moses were ended."

Nehemiah 1:4 "It came to pass, when I heard these words, that I sat down and wept, and mourned certain days, and fasted, and prayed before the God of heaven;"

Daniel 10:2 "In those days I Daniel was mourning three full weeks."

Other things can mourn besides people.

Isaiah 3:26 "Her gates shall lament and mourn; and she being desolate shall sit upon the ground."

Isaiah 24:4 "The earth mourneth and fadeth away;"

Isaiah 24:7 "The new wine mourneth, the vine languisheth, all the merry hearted do sigh."

Jeremiah 4:28 "For this shall the earth mourn, and the heavens above be black; because I have spoken it, I have purposed it;"

Jeremiah 12:4 "How long shall the land mourn, and the herbs of every field wither, for the wickedness of them that dwell therein?"

Jeremiah 23:10 "For the land is full of adulterers; for because of swearing the land mourneth; the pleasant places of the wilderness are dried up, and their course is evil, and their force is not right."

Joel 1:10 "The field is wasted, the land mourneth; for the corn is wasted: the new wine is dried up, the oil languisheth."

Additional examples of mourning:

Deuteronomy 26:14 "I have not eaten thereof in my mourning;"

Psalm 35:14 "I behaved myself as though he had been my friend or brother: I bowed down heavily, as one that mourneth for his mother."

Psalm 42:9 "I will say unto God my rock, Why hast thou forgotten me? why go I mourning because of the oppression of the enemy?"

Isaiah 59:11 "We roar all like bears, and mourn sore like doves:"

Lamentations 5:15 "The joy of our heart is ceased; our dance is turned into mourning."

28

I'm Ready to Process my Grief
What Can I Expect?

Over fifteen million people deal with loss each year and the grieving process is different for each person. Studies in human behavior show that similar to a baby growing into an adult, grief starts with infancy and develops through five typical stages: *denial, anger, bargaining, depression, and acceptance.* Grief is like an iceberg. Ninety percent of it is hidden underwater and can be almost impossible to measure or identify. It is an unusual experience and our hearts don't know exactly what to do with it.

Imagine a file cabinet inside of your heart that has a folder in it labeled "Disappointing Loss." It holds a variety of files, each representing an event where something familiar was changed. The files contain such a random collection of unexpected and disheartening moments that it is difficult to isolate each thought in each file.

Because our society often teaches suppression of feelings, many of our files have feelings connected to them that have never processed. Everyone is unique with their own unique files, but amazingly, our archives contain similar information. They contain the memories of the loss of things of value.

Grief work is actually *work*. You'll want a pen, paper (maybe a journal), and private space with no distraction (kids, cell phone, television, etc). Plan some blocks of time over a short period. Go at your own pace; be aware that when you pause, it may be a long time before you come back to this, so it's best to power through as much as you can. The Lord will help you. Psalm 18:28 tells us, *"For thou wilt light my candle: the LORD my God will enlighten my darkness."* Next you will find the *The Seven Steps to Healing*. Consider starting your journey now.

29

Seven Steps to Healing

1. Recognize and honor each visible loss. Take your time to think back to early childhood, as early as you can remember. You may need to close your eyes. Mentally walk through your youngest years, and each school year, and then each job you've held. Walk through each significant relationship you've been in. Allow hurtful events or words or losses to come back to your mind. Identify them on a list.

2. Identify past invisible losses. Go back through your life starting with your childhood. Ask the Lord to reveal the invisible losses that may have disillusioned you in life and may have been locked in your heart ungrieved all these years. Identify them on a list.

3. Look at each item on your list. Acknowledge the pain connected to each loss. Add in all connected feelings of grief.

4. You may have some soul ties connected to past pain; Use The Soul Tie Prayers in chapter thirty-nine.

5. Identify and break strongholds. Do this by praying The Stronghold Breaking Prayers starting in chapter forty-three.

6. After the first five steps, think back through your losses. Do any painful memories seem to stand out? You'll want to pray The Inner Healing Prayer in chapter forty.

7. Pray The Physical Healing Prayer (chapter forty-two). Also, occasionally, after completing *The Seven Steps to Healing,* there may be a strong, unusual feeling of discomfort that won't shake. If this is the case, The Deliverance Prayer might be needed (chapter forty-one).

Feeling like you need to do something practical? We all require private time to work things out in our mind and figure things out. Use the matching workbook where you'll find more stories, compelling questions, and a space to reflect and process.

30

Anointing with Oil

What type of oil do you use when you anoint? Many people use a *carrier* oil of some kind like olive oil. Carrier oils have large molecules that penetrate the surface of the skin slowly.

In my ministry opportunities, I have seen many types of oil used, and it all comes down to *preference*. My point is that you need to be flexible. Don't feel like there's only one type of anointing oil. Often I see olive oil or special oils from Israel being used. When it comes to the spiritual aspect of anointing, I don't think that the type of oil you use matters.

I once heard a pastor share that when he went to someone's house to anoint them, he forgot to bring his oil. All they had was motor oil, so he used it! (I don't think he knew about the chemicals in it.) I also know someone who was in a bind and needed to anoint. All she had was her chapstick. Both of these individuals used what they had and were successful in their anointing and prayer time.

You may wonder what I use when I anoint. I most often use *essential* oils. The molecules in essential oils are microscopic and penetrate our cells within seconds. When I anoint before prayer, I use Frankincense essential oil. It was used during Biblical times in the temples and has also been used throughout history in churches for its ability to clear the mind and improve spiritual awareness.

Other Biblical oils that I enjoy for prayer are cedarwood, cypress, myrrh, and hyssop. There have been documented uses of essential oils for physical health, as well as mental and emotional wellbeing. A fantastic option for emotional wellness is Jasmine which is useful in uplifting and bringing about a sense of relaxation. It has long been included in skin care products and the petals collected for tea.

In reading through the scriptures, it makes sense why the wise men would have presented baby Jesus with the precious gift of frankincense which was comparable in value to gold. If you're a researcher like me, there is a wonderful book on the subject called *Essential Oils of the Bible* written by Dr. David Stewart. In his book, Dr. Stewart documents hundreds of times that oils are mentioned in the Bible. My husband and I have had the opportunity to meet him and were touched by his sincerity, gentleness, and love. For specific details on what we use, see the miscellaneous information section at the end of the book.

Let's Do It!
Layers of Healing

31

Stronghold Breaking

Is shifting out of a negative emotional state difficult for you? Do you get pulled into the emotional perimeter of those around you? Do you find yourself repeatedly responding in the same negative patterns to some situations regardless of your best intentions to do otherwise? Do your feelings or negative emotions seem to be beyond your control?

I recently heard a story from an eighty-eight-year-old cancer-stricken, lonely Jewish man who had believed he was a failure his whole life. He had tried hard in the fourth grade to pass, but had failed, and had never recovered his self-confidence. He began to believe the enemy's lies. *Everyone else is smarter than you. There's no use in trying; you'll just fail. You'll never be successful. You're stupid. You're dumb. Forget about having a good future. You're going to fail at everything you try. Your life is a total failure.* This senior had held onto unforgiveness against himself for over eighty years.

As we know, God does not make failures. *"You are not a failure,"* I told the man. *"The problem is that you have believed a lie all these years. Let's get rid of this stronghold of failure." "I am too old! I am eighty-eight, and I have believed this my whole life"* he responded.

One thing I know about strongholds is that they do not like to be addressed. They have every excuse in the world, however the Bible directs us to *pull down* strongholds. The man jumped up to get his dictionary. He wanted to know the definition of a stronghold.

His dictionary defined it as "an area of predominance." I told the man, *"You do not need to live with this stronghold one more day. Let's tear it down!"* and he agreed.

The Bible says, *"Confess your faults one to another, pray for one another, and you will be healed."* He wasn't sure how to tear down a stronghold, so I led him in a simple declaration. *"I confess believing the lie that I was a failure. I confess believing the lie that I would never be successful and that I was stupid and I renounce its hold on my life."* The Lord showed us some pictures of what the stronghold looked like and we saw it being torn down. I prayed, *"I tear down this stronghold and I ask You Lord to place Your truth where these lies have been."* We then trusted God that his work had been done. I knew positive changes would follow.

When strongholds are torn down, the old way of thinking is removed and taken away; it is destroyed. God then replaces the old way of thinking with new thoughts based on His Word and based in truth.

Later in the day, the man shared that he had never had a talk like that with anyone. He wondered how he would be able to stop the negative habit of believing he was stupid. I reminded him that when the stronghold was torn down, the old way of thinking along with the bad habits had miraculously been removed by God. Stronghold breaking is as huge of a miracle as a physical healing.

I told the man that after it was pulled down, that God had placed within his mind, a new way of thinking, based in truth. I reassured him that he would be positively affected.

Sure enough, after some time had passed, the man observed that he was not struggling with continual thoughts of failure. He passed away a little under a year later, confidant in overcoming his years of self-doubt.

If you know anyone who may have a stronghold of *failure*, you can find the steps to break it in chapter forty-six. I have seen miracles in the lives of those I know, over and over again in the area of stronghold breaking. God's design is for us to be whole. His plan is for us to be healed from our past and to move forward, helping those around us, and seeking after the things of God.

Strongholds are frustrating and discouraging. They prevent forward movement, forgiveness, and functional, healthy relationships. A stronghold is a spiritual fortress made of wrong thoughts; a fortified dwelling place which operates in power against us. Strongholds are based on lies that challenge Biblical truth.

Fundamentally, a stronghold is a block that prevents individuals from seeing the world accurately. It's a strong influence, a grip, negative pattern, persistent oppression, obsession, hindrance, or harassment.

If you answered yes to any of the questions at the beginning of this chapter, you probably need to break strongholds.

<u>Below I will walk you through ten steps to breaking a stronghold.</u>

1. The first step is to be sure of your personal salvation. Romans 10:9 is clear that if you confess with your mouth and believe in your heart that Jesus Christ is Lord, you will be saved. Receiving salvation starts with believing in your heart that Jesus is Lord, and then speaking out loud that Jesus Christ is Lord. If you have not received salvation or are not sure if you are saved, you can pray a simple prayer like this: *"Dear Lord I repent for the sins of my past. I believe that Jesus Christ is Lord. I give my life to you, and I put my life in your hands. In Jesus name, Amen."*

2. The second step is to fill out the Breaking Negative Patterns Identification Form. You can find it at the end of the book. Decide how frequently you encounter each symptom. Score yourself based on a scale where five is extremely frequent, and zero is never. This will identify the strongholds in your life.

3. Decide which strongholds to break. In the back of the book you will find a list of the strongholds from each book in the series. They each contain different strongholds.

4. Start breaking strongholds. You can find different strongholds towards the back of each book in the series. Take your time listing the symptoms. Speaking your confessions *out loud* is necessary. There are principles in God's word that have led us to this conclusion, and we also believe that the stronghold needs to hear your voice as you confess and renounce its hold on you and your family line. I John 1:9 tells us, *"If we confess our sins, he is faithful and just to forgive us our sins, and to cleanse us from all unrighteousness."* To break a stronghold, speak the words, *"I confess..."* and then verbally list each symptom.

5. After confessing the symptoms of a stronghold, add "I confess this for myself, my parents, my grandparents, my great grandparents and all of my ancestors back to Adam, and I renounce its hold on my life and on my family line." You'll find this noted at the end of each stronghold in the back. We do this to spiritually clean our bloodline for sin that has never been repented for. There is more on this topic in *Breaking Negative Patterns*.

6. After each stronghold and the symptoms have been confessed, take one to two minutes to listen. Ask the Lord to show you if there is anything attached to the symptoms. Be intentional about thoroughly waiting to see what He shows you for each stronghold. If a word comes, consider confessing it. If a memory comes, confess anything negative connected to it.

7. Ask the Lord to show you what the stronghold looks like. For me, I usually see something different than the last stronghold that was broken. Sometimes it looks like a tower, other times a dead tree or root, other times a high wall, etc. If someone is with you or you're breaking strongholds as a group, work as a team. Each person should share all things that come to mind, even if they don't make sense, because every thought will be meaningful.

8. Ask the Lord to break it. He may show you a tool (like a sledgehammer or axe) or might send a wind or something from nature to destroy it. It may be pulled down, broken, smashed, or destroyed. See the stronghold as an object being torn down.

9. Ask the Lord to replace it with something new. Be in the moment. Experience what He does!

10. Pray The Stronghold Breaking Prayer in chapter forty-three.

If you need a deeper understanding of what they are, how they operate, and how to break them, read the first book in this series, *Breaking Negative Patterns*. It is mainly about strongholds, and it will take you step-by-step through the process.

32

Seven Steps to Breaking Soul Ties

"For the LORD shall be thine everlasting light, and the days of thy mourning shall be ended." (Isaiah 60:20)

Soul ties must be strategically broken in order to release two people's hearts from one another; they do not automatically dissolve when a relationship does. Releasing soul ties helps grievers who are suffering. It gets to the core of the loss, so the griever can go on to lead a happy and healthy life.

Q: After I break a soul tie, do I need to let the person know?

A: No, you don't. Breaking a soul tie is a personal decision. It's between you and God.

Consider allowing the Lord to shine light on your past and present relationships. If names or faces come to mind, you'll want to break soul ties one at a time. You'll know that your heart needs to break a soul tie if you feel a cautious hesitation of distrust, rejection, or sadness when you think about a particular person or memory.

Seven Steps to Soul Tie Breaking:

1. *Confess and ask Forgiveness.*
2. *Renounce (reject and abandon old ways).*
3. *Cut Ties.*
4. *Release.*
5. *Bind assignments against you from the enemy.*
6. *Cleanse and Restore.*
7. *Bless.*

Chapter thirty-nine will walk you through this process and covers all seven of these steps. As you pray this prayer, picture a hook gently being pulled out of your heart and a hook also leaving the other person's heart. Visualize the soul tie being severed in the spirit (like a scissor snip of a fishing line connecting both parties). You will want to pray this prayer aloud each time you break a soul tie.

33

The Path of Light
The Beauty of Inner Healing

Krista was only five when her stepmother came upstairs to tell her that her father had passed away in the night. Her stepmother didn't sit with her or comfort her or answer any questions. Krista was left alone for what seemed like days as she tried to process what her stepmother had said. She had never felt so alone. She was scared and had no one to talk to.

Fast forward twenty-five years, and Krista is learning about inner healing. The process sounds intriguing and seems easy enough. She has no idea if she needs inner healing, but figures it won't hurt to try. She clears an hour of her schedule and finds a quiet spot. She shuts off her phone and closes her eyes, asking the Lord to shine His holy light on her memories. Instantly, she sees her five-year-old self, sitting upstairs on her bed.

She sees her stepmother come in and share the news and then walk out. Feelings begin to flood back... *sadness, loneliness, abandonment, helplessness, fear*.

Krista sees her five-year-old self crying and realizes that she has a wound she's been carrying her whole life. She knows she needs inner healing and is ready to start.

Krista knows what she's feeling. She speaks aloud, *"I confess holding onto sadness, helplessness, fear, loneliness, and abandonment and I renounce its hold on my life. I confess holding onto unforgiveness and bitterness toward my stepmother for being cold and uncaring... for not comforting me in my deepest need."*

Krista asks Jesus to show her where He was when she was crying on her bed alone. Krista sees Jesus in her memory. He's in the room sitting on the bed next to the five-year-old version of her. His hand is on her shoulder and He's grieving with her. Krista feels comforted as she sees Jesus put His arm around her and hold her near.

She realizes that she was not alone in that room. All these years she had remembered herself being alone, but the truth was that Jesus had been there with her. She sees Jesus wiping away her tears, and she feels comforted as she focuses on being wrapped in the warmth of His love.

She asks the Lord to fill her heart with peace. She breathes deeply and watches in her mind until Jesus takes her by the hand and leads her out of the dark room, closing the door gently behind her. Krista is not sure where they go, but she is keenly aware of a new sense of relief. She pushes the picture of her in her old bedroom up to heaven and sees herself putting the image of the event in God's hands. There is peace where there used to be pain. The memory finishes, and she feels closure for the first time. She has been crying cleansing tears throughout the experience, and she feels light and calm.

Inner healing is the healing of the heart; the healing of feelings and emotions. It's a process in which we go back to a painful memory and invite Jesus into it. It's a very healing experience and those who have gone through it report a peaceful, light feeling of comfort that takes the place of the negative or heavy feelings of the past. The memory then loses its power, grip, and influence over us and our thoughts.

Seven Steps to Inner Healing:

1. Inner healing involves getting alone with the Lord and having an encounter with the presence of God. In I Kings 19:13, when Elijah was hearing the voice of the Lord and was preparing to experience His presence, he purposefully wrapped his face in his mantle. To start, remove all distractions. *Anoint yourself and pray The Inner Healing Prayer in chapter forty.*

2. Once you have a quiet spot, ask God to shine His light on any experiences or events from the past that have been hurtful. He may remind you of memories and show you past experiences. *"We have also a more sure word of prophecy; whereunto ye do well that ye take heed, as unto a light that shineth in a dark place, until the day dawn, and the day star arise in your hearts."* (2 Peter 1:19) Close your eyes and see the situation in your mind. Go back to the location. You may need to wait a few moments until you can see it in your mind. It might be tricky at first, but you'll get the hang of it.

3. Allow the Lord to reveal negative feelings you have not processed from the experience. As they come, confess what you've been holding onto *"I confess fear, bitterness, doubt, etc."* Confess negative behaviors or patterns you've adopted to escape those feelings.

4. Forgive each person connected with the experience. Mark 11:25 states, *"And when ye stand praying, forgive, if ye have ought against any: that your Father also which is in heaven may forgive you your trespasses."*

5. Now ask Jesus where He was in the picture. With your eyes still closed, wait for Him to show you where He was. *Invite Jesus into the memory.* Watch what happens. Watch what Jesus does. Enjoy the experience of being with Him. Let Him comfort you. Let Him be all you needed. *"He shall feed his flock like a shepherd: he shall gather the lambs with his arm, and carry them in his bosom, and shall gently lead those that are with young."* (Isaiah 40:11)

6. See yourself pushing the scenario up to heaven. I like to see myself handing the situation to God. Push it up again if you need to. See the Lord reaching down and taking it from you. *"Cast thy burden upon the Lord, and he shall sustain thee: he shall never suffer the righteous to be moved."* (Psalm 55:22)

7. Ask the Lord to bring the next memory that needs to be healed and repeat steps two through six. This is the process of Inner Healing. When no more memories come to your mind, ask God to cleanse and heal your memories. Intentionally breathe in the atmosphere of heaven. See peace filling every inch of your mind, body, and soul.

34

Deliverance
Q & A

"For we wrestle not against flesh and blood, but against principalities, against powers, against the rulers of the darkness of this world, against spiritual wickedness in high places." (Ephesians 6:12)

Last night, as I was working with a family to break strongholds, after anointing each member of the family (we used frankincense essential oil) and confessing the symptoms of the stronghold of *anger*, one of the children saw a picture of a cheetah with angry eyes. She described his eyes and added the words *hatred, murder, and revenge.*

While breaking strongholds, if a person sees an animal or being that looks dark, scary, or projects negative emotion in the eyes, it's worth noting. Once someone saw a shadow covered in a cape holding a sickle. We discerned that it was a spirit of death and recognized that the Lord was revealing a demonic spirit that needed to be addressed.

John Eckhardt has a book called *The Demon Hit List* which is helpful in identifying their names. *Identifying spirits by name* is a key to having authority over them and commanding them to go. Thankfully, there is nothing of which to be afraid. The spirit of fear is nothing more than a tiny mouse with a megaphone. Jesus has given us the power to overcome the strategy of the enemy against us.

I knew to jot down the words that the child saw in the cheetah's eyes because they represented the names of demons that the Lord was helping us to identify. I would need this list when we were done with stronghold breaking. After stronghold breaking was complete, I then encouraged the family to be intentional for the next few minutes about breathing out anger, hatred, murder, and revenge and breathing in the atmosphere of heaven. I did deliverance in an authoritative and straightforward way.

I simply said, *"I take authority over anger, hatred, murder, revenge, and sabotage and I bind you right now in Jesus' name. I command you to loose your hold and go to the feet of Jesus to be dealt with by Him. I loose angels to help drag these things out. All demonic oppression, you **go** right now, in Jesus' name! God, I ask that you would fill us with Your Holy Spirit, and that You would touch us with Your anointing. I ask that You would pour it from heaven like oil. Fill us up tangibly like an empty vessel being filled. Fill us from the bottom of our feet up through our legs, through our hips, up to our shoulders, through our arms, and up into our mind, Lord Jesus. I pray that You would fill us anew with the fresh fire of God and the power of Your Holy Spirit in Jesus' name, Amen."* The Deliverance Prayer can be found ahead in chapter forty-one.

Q: Can a Christian have a demon?

A: I believe that Christians can be oppressed by demonic spirits (demons) at times in their lives, but not necessarily possessed. Many times I have seen deliverance follow soul tie breaking, inner healing, or stronghold breaking. Demons like to be in the pain, and once the pain is gone they become restless.

Binding the strongman and casting out demons is not usually a Sunday morning sermon and I don't go into much detail in this book regarding deliverance. However, I can recommend a practical and valuable guide to spiritual warfare called *Delivering the Captives: Understanding the Strongman and How to Defeat Him* by Alice Smith. This manual provides sound Biblical instruction for identifying, binding, and casting out demonic spirits.

<u>Take The Deliverance Quiz to find out if there's a chance you could be demonically oppressed.</u>

1. Do your emotions widely vary from 0 to 10 on specific topics?

2. Do you say or do hurtful things of which you have no memory?

3. Do people tell you that you are antagonistic, controlling, spiteful, cold, hard, belittling, disrespectful, dismissive, divisive, or prideful?

4. Do you surprise yourself by responding to situations differently than you expected?

5. Do you often feel spiritually defeated? (You are prayed over and feel temptation or oppression lift just to find it back the next day?)

6. Do things bother you a lot?

7. Do you feel frustrated, hurt, or offended often?

8. Are you dissatisfied often?

9. Do you have overpowering carnal or sinful habits?

10. Do you wake up grumpy for no reason?

11. Do you think there's a good chance that a door has been opened somewhere and a demonic spirit has been given a legal right into your life?

12. Are you pessimistic, judging, or quick to accuse?

13. Do you recognize that you feel negative or give off a negative vibe but don't know what to do about it?

14. Is your mind a constant battleground?

If you answered yes to three or more of these questions, you may need deliverance from demonic oppression. Also, if you have broken soul ties and strongholds and have done inner healing and you still sense a continuous agitation or anxiety, there's a good chance you'll want to pray the self-deliverance prayer in chapter forty-one.

Q: Is deliverance really something I can do?

A: Yes! In Mark 16:17, it says *"And these signs shall follow them that believe; In my name shall they cast out devils; they shall speak with new tongues."* The enemy realizes you are walking in your authority, and he is wanting to hold you back. He wants to keep you stagnant and thinking only about yourself. He knows the impact that you can have on others when you begin to step into the full understanding of your identity and authority in Christ, and it scares him. Your spiritual growth and development give *him* anxiety.

Q: Is prayer and fasting a good idea before I start?

A: Absolutely. In Mark 9:29 Jesus tells us that certain types of spirits can only come forth by prayer and fasting. It was after Jesus fasted, that he was victorious over the enemy and his power.

Q: Can spirits come back after they have been cast out?

A: Freedom and healing must be maintained. Chapter thirty-six contains helpful strategies. When your life is filled with the presence of God, demonic spirits will not be able to come back and bring any others with them. The Bible refers to a house being *swept clean or filled* after a person has been set free, which refers to filling yourself with scripture from God's Word and keeping your mind and body pure. If a spirit does regain entrance through sin, you can confess the sin and take authority over the demonic spirit and command it to go as soon as you recognize what has happened.

Q: Can a parent do deliverance on their child?

A: Absolutely. Parents have been given spiritual authority in their home, and the enemy knows that. If a parent understands their spiritual position and discerns that their child is demonically oppressed, they can take authority over the spirit, bind it, and command it to go.

Specific parental prayer for this can be found in The Deliverance Prayer chapter in the *When the Heart Won't Let Go Workbook*. If a child is of the age of understanding, they must desire to be free. If their desire is to stay in darkness, they will most likely open doors again to the enemy which can be detrimental. The Bible says that if a person goes back into their sin after going through deliverance, that the end result can be seven times worse than before. Jesus speaks about this topic in Matthew 12:43-45.

Q: Is it possible to do deliverance or break a stronghold off of someone without their knowledge?

A: It depends on the age. Yes for a child; it is possible for a parent to do deliverance and break strongholds off of a young child, or for another adult to do it with the parent's permission. The parent would need to repent of the things that have allowed the stronghold to be there. No, for an adult. It is *not* possible to do deliverance or break strongholds on an adult without their knowledge. Those of the age of understanding must verbally confess and break strongholds so that they can get set free and be delivered.

Q: Will I need to do deliverance more than once?

A: Some people get miraculously delivered all at once, whereas others find that it is a journey. You may find yourself walking in daily deliverance for a while until you are completely set free. Sometimes deliverance is a season and a process that can take time. Additionally, you may want support in your journey of deliverance through prayer sessions or a meeting with an experienced spiritual prayer warrior.

35

Physical Healing
Q & A

Q: Can illness be connected to grief?

A: Yes. Symptoms of grief often appear in the physical body and may include muscle knots, back problems, anxiety, and panic. Individuals who grieve often complain of exhaustion and heaviness in their lungs.

Q: Can illness be connected to stress?

A: Yes. Approximately 75% of doctor visits are due to mysterious stress-related conditions. It has been said by ministers that there are two approaches to praying for trauma or stress-induced sickness. They can pray for necks, backs, and other illnesses brought on by stress such as irritable bowel syndrome, acid reflux, ulcers, Crohn's disease, heart attacks, strokes, high blood pressure, diabetes, ulcers, and sleep apnea; *or* they can tell you how to get rid of stress, and you won't have to pray over those illnesses again.

Dr. Philip Gold was among speakers of a conference of the International Society for Neuro-Immune

Modulation. These experts study the effects of stress and depression on disease. Dr. Gold presented a study of bone density among twenty-six 40-year-old women; half of the women suffering from depression and half with normal emotional states. The depressed women all had high levels of stress hormones. Those with depression had bone density like that of a 70-year-old woman. They were at risk of fracture, and the magnitude of bone loss was surprising. What was the root? *Emotional Stress.*[4]

Many of our physical health issues are rooted in negative thought patterns or *strongholds* that have been locked into our cell memory. Almost any time an individual suffers from a physical condition, chronic or acute, something has happened in the past, perhaps even the distant past that could be the root cause of the condition.

There is a lot of power in the willingness to become humbly self-aware. I know of a woman who was diagnosed with cancer and was prompted to forgive someone but refused. Over several years, the cancer-stricken individual became weaker and eventually died. Their family was very sad and had often wondered if the bitterness was at the root of their disease.

The truth is, physical healing often follows healing of the heart. When the painful events, trauma, and feelings can be identified, its power can be broken, and the person will be released from carrying the load. Sleep will be better, the body will seem lighter, and the individual will feel happier.

---

[4] www.latimes.com/archives/la-xpm-19911-16-mn-65323-story.html

36

Maintaining Healing
Seven Ways to Stay Free

"And be not conformed to this world: but be ye transformed by the renewing of your mind, that ye may prove what is that good, and acceptable, and perfect, will of God." (Romans 12:2)

It is important to note that after healing, temptation will come to draw a person who is no longer a slave back into captivity. Freedom must be courageously maintained and protected in the time that follows.

Whenever temptation presents itself, the free captive must reject the darts of the enemy, stand firm, and declare that they are set free. Wholeness must be maintained and there are ways to maintain freedom.

Seven Things you can do to Stay Free:

1. Toxic people who are pushy or confrontational must have limited access to you.

2. Renew your mind by reading or listening to the Bible. Philippians 4:8 tells us, *"Whatsoever things are true, whatsoever things are honest, whatsoever things are just, whatsoever things are pure, whatsoever things are lovely, whatsoever things are of good report; if there be any virtue, and if there be any praise, think on these things."* Discipline the mind to these values.

3. Keep your heart from sin. Be quick to apologize and quick to forgive.

4. Don't make commitments out of pressure.

5. Resist the devil and take every thought captive. 2 Corinthians 10:5 states, *"Casting down imaginations, and every high thing that exalteth itself against the knowledge of God, and bringing into captivity every thought to the obedience of Christ."* God calls us to take every thought captive to the obedience of Christ. Whenever a thought comes into my mind that doesn't feel right to me, I say, *"I take authority over you, and I bind you in Jesus' name."* I picture the thought being rejected and pushed up to God's throne. After that, it's usually not in my mind at all anymore. If it tries to creep back in, I do this three-second process again.

6. Be quick to practice The Seven Life-Changing Prayers ahead as the need arises.

7. Sing to the Lord. Singing slows your breathing and lowers the production of stress hormones in as little as ten minutes. It also produces vibrations that increase the brain's production of endorphins *(Indiana Univ., South Bend)*. *"A merry heart doeth good like a medicine: but a broken spirit drieth the bones."* (Proverbs 17:22)

Seven Life-Changing Prayers

37

Listening Prayer

Have you ever wondered *How can I hear God's voice clearly?* Listening Prayer is the key to using the power of being still, to see in the spirit. Lester Sumrall once said that prayer is the council chamber where divine commands are issued, and solutions are generated through the divine power of God. Listening Prayer will help you hear the many ways that God speaks. It's a wonderful way to spend quiet time with the Lord.

Seven Steps to Listening Prayer:

1. Find a quiet and private atmosphere; No distractions.

2. Take authority over and bind distraction, confusion, deception, doubt, and unbelief. Do it by saying, *"I take authority over all distraction, confusion, deception, doubt, and unbelief and I bind you in Jesus' name."*

3. Quiet your heart to be open to hearing from God. "Lord, please speak to me." The young prophet,

Samuel did this when he prayed, *"Speak Lord, for Your servant is listening."*

4. Listen to receive what God wants to show you. Do not make any sounds with your mouth. You aren't listening if you are talking; note that it may be uncomfortable at first. We all could learn to develop the discipline to be still. *"Be still, and know that I am God: I will be exalted among the heathen, I will be exalted in the earth."* (Psalm 46:10)

5. When you get an impression or a picture, watch the image evolve. It often unfolds like a movie. As you continue to watch what is happening, the Lord may start to download revelation.

6. When something comes to you no matter how big or small, write it down. Journaling will help you get the most out of the experience.

7. Be aware of words, memories, ideas, or other things that come to your mind. Generally, when we set time aside to hear from the Lord, the thoughts that come to mind are from Him and are meant to move us in a particular direction. If you are unsure why something is coming, ask the Lord about it. He might give you a scripture or remind you of something. He may unfold a memory or a scene. Be vigilant with thoughts that come. You might need to confess holding onto the belief, the emotion, or the feeling that the thought evoked. You may need to push the picture up to Him. At the same time, don't get so caught up in trying to figure out something, that you close yourself off to the next thing the Lord wants to reveal or speak to you.

38

The Protection Prayer

"I the LORD have called thee in righteousness, and will hold thine hand, and will keep thee." (Isaiah 42:6)

It's my heart's desire to provide the tools necessary for you to take hold of your own liberty and freedom; to learn to use your authority in Christ Jesus. This way, any time the enemy begins to press in, you know that you can stand and resist him, and he will have to flee.

Do you believe that God wants to use you to help others? The training process is simple. You are holding the tool in your hand. God has already given you the authority and placed you in your circle of influence, which is unique to any other sphere of influence on earth. I encourage you to move ahead with your personal healing and then take others through the process.

The steps are so easy, and anyone who knows their authority can walk others through it. Take your friends and family through the steps in this book. Get them a copy or download the Kindle version on Amazon for them so they can start soon. Use the *Negative Pattern Identification Form* in the back, the lists, and the prayers to guide you as you help others get set free.

The prayers you'll need are in the pages ahead. I have provided the following prayers, not as a formula, but as a sample to demonstrate the application of truth through prayer. As you seek the Holy Spirit for direction He will guide your prayers, and you will receive healing and deliverance in your life.

The Protection Prayer

"I pray Your protection over myself. I put on my helmet of salvation, my breastplate of righteousness, my belt of truth, my shoes of peace and I pick up my sword of the spirit and my shield of faith. Surround me with Your Presence and the atmosphere of heaven. I pray wisdom and revelation for myself and strength, joy, power, and desire to do Your will. I ask You Lord to release Your angelic host to minister to me and to stand guard around me and my home in Jesus' name, Amen."

39

The Soul Tie Prayers

When breaking a soul tie, be sure to pray the following Soul Tie Prayer. You'll want to fill in the blanks with the person's name who you are breaking the soul tie with. Take your time. Don't skip words or sentences and pray aloud.

"I confess all ungodly soul ties that I've entered into. I confess unforgiveness toward myself and ___. I confess all deception, confusion, accusation, and ruminations between myself and ___. I confess idolatry, injustice, malice, and manipulation and I ask You, Lord, to forgive me. I renounce and break all vows and promises between myself and ___. I cut all spiritual ropes and ties that bind me to them in Jesus' name. I ask You, Lord, to reach down with Your hand and cut the connection in the spirit between us. I release all negative memories that are connected to ___. I release myself from ___, and I release him/her from me. I take back every part of myself that I have given away emotionally, physically, relationally, and spiritually. I release every part of them and send it

back to them. I take authority over the strategy of the enemy to maintain this negative soul tie, and I bind it in Jesus' name. I take authority over all demonic assignments against me to keep me discouraged, deceived, controlled, or in bondage. Pour out Your blood and cleanse me from the top of my head to the bottom of my feet. Cleanse my spirit, soul, and body and restore me to wholeness. I thank You, Lord, for the development that You've done in my life because of this person. I release them, and I send them off with a blessing now in Jesus' name, Amen."

If you need to cut a soul tie for one or more of the following specific reasons, include the additional prayer(s) below.

Prolonged Grief over a Death

"I confess prolonged grief, guilt, and regret. Thank You for the blessing ____ was to my life. I break any negative soul ties that I had with ____. Please cleanse my memories. Take any negative memories I have from my time with them and seal the memories that should stay with me. I release my loved one to You. Please fill the hole and heal the pain in my heart. I ask You, God, to send mighty angels to cover me and Your Holy Spirit to comfort me. Release Your joy to replace my mourning in Jesus' name."

Breakups

"Thank You for the blessing that ___ was to my life. I confess holding on to grief, sadness, hurt, and pain. I confess all rejection, discouragement, guilt, and regret. I take back every piece of my heart that was given away. I

ask You, Lord, to heal me and restore me. I release ___ to You, and I bless him/her now in Jesus' name."

Codependent, Controlling, Dysfunctional Relationships

"Lord, I pray that You would release me from all dysfunction and demonic control that has harassed me. Cleanse me and protect me from being involved in toxic relationships in the future. I take authority over, and I bind all demonic spirits that have tormented me and have caused guilt or shame. I take authority over, and I bind all demonic spirits of jealousy, confusion, and frustration. I take authority over, and I bind all demonic spirits of witchcraft and control sent with assignments to maintain ungodly soul ties. Release me, Lord, and cover me in the blood of Jesus. I ask that You would restore my mind and give me joy, wisdom, hope, and discernment in Jesus' name."

Sexual Encounters

"I confess all impurity, addiction, sexual sin, and sexual soul ties for myself and for the generations that have come before me. I renounce its hold on my life and on my family line. I confess broken covenants and ask You, Lord, to break all unholy contracts and covenants that I've signed with my words or actions. I take back all pieces of myself that were given away. I ask You to cleanse me completely, in Jesus' name."

Cults (where there have been soul ties with a deceptive or controlling organization or religion)

"And what concord hath Christ with Belial? or what part hath he that believeth with an infidel? And what

agreement hath the temple of God with idols?" (2 Corinthians 6:15-16)

"I confess involvement with all belief systems that are not based on the Bible, which is God's truth. I confess and break all ungodly promises, declarations, deceptions, and vows that I've made in my heart, my mind, or with my mouth, and I renounce them on my life and on my family line. I confess partaking in any belief systems influenced by the spirit of Antichrist and all beliefs I've taken on because of it. I confess submitting to lies, darkness, heaviness, idolatry, control, and oppression. Please cleanse me, Lord, of the debris and residue of idolatry. I release myself from the cult or organization of ____ and I declare today that I submit my life to God and to His holy calling. I pray that Your truth will penetrate every part of me in Jesus' name."

False Accusation and Betrayal

"Lord, I come to You with the hurt of accusation and betrayal. I break the power of every negative word curse that has been spoken over me or behind my back. I use the sword of the Spirit to cut off all anxiety, guilt, shame, and condemnation. I pull out every dart of judgment and every dagger of betrayal and accusation. I release the people who did this to me. I bless them and I lift them up to Your throne. I pray that You would heal my heart of the wounds of this trauma in Jesus' name."

Loss of a Pet

"I thank You, Lord, for the blessing and comfort that ____ was to me. I release all negative thoughts, feelings, or memories that I have when I think about him/her

including guilt, condemnation, regret, sadness, confusion, anger, hurt, and pain. I release myself from ___, and I release him/her from me. I picture ___ going up to You as You sit on Your throne. I pray that You would fill every void in my heart with Your light and that You would be my comfort, in Jesus' name."

Cleansing of an Ongoing Relationship

In a situation where you must continue in a relationship with someone, and you feel that the link needs to be cleansed spiritually, picture the Lord scrubbing the cable or line between you and the other person. See Him removing all of the negative debris as you pray this prayer:

"I confess all ungodly soul ties that I've entered into with ___. Lord, I ask that You would cleanse the soul tie between myself and ___. I confess all negative words or thoughts that I've spoken or projected over them, and I break off all projections, evil thoughts, or word curses that they've spoken over me. I confess unforgiveness toward myself and ___. I confess all deception, confusion, accusation, and ruminations between myself and ___. I confess idolatry, injustice, control, and manipulation and I ask You, Lord, to forgive me. I renounce and break all vows and promises between myself and ___. I cut all ropes and ties that bind me to ___ in Jesus' name. I ask You, Lord, to reach down with Your hand and cut any negative connection in the spirit between us. I release all negative memories that are connected to ___. I take authority over every strategy of the enemy to maintain negative ties, and I bind it in Jesus' name. I take

authority over every demonic assignment against me to keep me discouraged, deceived, controlled, or in bondage. I ask You, Lord, to cleanse the tie between us. Remove the negative and strengthen the positive. Thank You, Lord, for cleansing our relationship. Pour out Your blood and cleanse me from the top of my head to the bottom of my feet. Cleanse my spirit, my soul, and my body and restore me to wholeness. I thank You, Lord, for the development that You've done in me because of this person. I submit them to You, now. I release myself from them, and I release them from me with a blessing in Jesus' name."

40

The Inner Healing Prayer

"For God, who commanded the light to shine out of darkness, hath shined in our hearts, to give the light of the knowledge of the glory of God in the face of Jesus Christ." (2 Corinthians 4:6)

First, anoint yourself with oil. Did you know that there are oils of joy and gladness that are mentioned in the Bible? Throughout the scriptures, we read of odors, fragrances, ointments, aromas, perfumes, and sweet savors that rejoice the heart.

The Lord placed plants on the earth for us, and the natural properties found in them produce a soothing, uplifting effect on the mind and emotions, bringing balance to the body. When an essential oil is diffused, or applied topically, the results foster a sense of emotional balance and well-being.

Chapter thirty-three included the steps for Inner Healing. Place your hands on your head and heart. Meditate on God's Presence and breathe in peace. Be infused with the atmosphere of heaven as you pray the following prayer.

"I speak, 'Peace, be still' to the turbulence in my life, my heart, and my thoughts. Peace to my thinking. Peace to my heart. I cover my mind with the helmet of salvation. Lord, help my mind to stay upon You. I pray healing over my heart, my mind, my will, and my emotions and I thank You that you are cleansing and healing my memories. I speak to all parts of myself to become one. I thank You, Lord, for wholeness in every area of my life. I reaffirm my trust in You, and I choose to forgive myself of all guilt and regret. I ask You to release life to every cell, every thought, and every part of my body. Pour out the oil of Your presence. I receive the fire of Your presence Father, the fire that burns and releases a passion for You. In Jesus' name, Amen."

41

The Deliverance Prayer

"The thief cometh not, but for to steal, and to kill, and to destroy: I am come that they might have life, and that they might have it more abundantly." (John 10:10)

In James 4:7, the Bible says *to resist the devil and he will flee.* If the enemy tries to shoot darts of fear and intimidation before you start The Deliverance Prayer, then pray this:

"Lord, I thank You that I do not have any fear in dealing with the enemy and demons because You have given me power over all the schemes of the enemy. Your Word promises me that nothing will hurt me. I am not at a disadvantage and I declare that I am not in fear of the enemy. Thank You for helping me understand my authority and identity and for helping me to see myself the way that You see me. By faith, I acknowledge the protection of Your blood. I see You pouring out Your blood over my life, my home, my family, and all of my possessions. Thank You, Lord, for Your protection through the blood of Jesus, Amen."

Ten Steps to Deliverance

1. Anoint with oil.

2. Break Strongholds. Demonic spirits can be challenging to evict if they have a stronghold to live in.

3. Experience Inner Healing. It is often challenging to get a demon out of an emotional wound unless inner healing and stronghold breaking have first occurred.

4. Take notes of any dark figures or darkly colored animals that appear. Document the sensations and thoughts that accompany them. They will usually have scary eyes or project a strong, unsettling feeling. The impressions or feelings that come along with them is often the names of the spirits you'll be addressing (fear, death, etc.) *They project what they are.* If nothing comes to you, think about how it makes you feel. Use the list of symptoms under the stronghold. That will be the clue to their name. Their name is what they project. For example, fear projects fear. If the picture is of a dark animal, they may even be moving quickly to attack. Don't let this scare you. Just know that this is the nature of evil spirits.

*5. Boldly and audibly speak these words: "I take authority over ____ (fill in the blank with the name of the spirit(s) you have discerned; if you aren't sure, continue the prayer anyway) and I bind you right now in Jesus' name. All demonic oppression, you **go** right now in Jesus' name. I **command** you to loose your hold and go to the feet of Jesus to be dealt with by Him. I take authority over every unclean thing that has taken* *advantage of my vulnerability and my weaknesses. I confess all unconfessed sin, and I renounce every demonic spirit known or unknown. I refuse to accept your influence in my life. Every place you have influenced my decisions, every place you've manipulated my actions, I **command** you to leave those areas now. Your right to stay has been broken, and you **must** leave me now. I loose angels to help drag these things out. I ask You, Lord, to deliver me and let Your perfect love cast out every demonic thing. I ask that You would fill me with Your Holy Spirit and that You would touch me with Your anointing. I thank You that the anointing breaks every yoke of bondage. I ask that You would pour it from heaven like oil, filling me completely. I pray that You would fill me with fresh fire and the power of your Holy Spirit in Jesus' name."*

6. Sit quietly and intentionally breathe out. If any impressions come to you, command those to go. Say, "I take authority over ___ , and I bind you" to whatever comes to you. Breathe out several times (through your mouth). It is like expelling toxic air (evil spirits).

*7. Declare out loud to the enemy, "Devil, you have no place in me and no power over me. I will no longer listen to your voice and succumb to your suggestions. I will no longer entertain images that you place in my mind. I will no longer listen to the lies. I close all of the doors of my life to you. I **command** all fear, confusion, and thoughts that release insecurity to be silent in Jesus' name. I **command** every unholy word* *and thought to fall to the ground. The blood of Jesus Christ is against you, Satan! I renounce you, and I* **command** *you to leave my being, spirit, soul, and body. I declare that the chains are falling, they are BROKEN by the blood of Jesus and by the authority of His Name. I command peace where there has been agitation and rest where there has been anxiety. I receive the peace of God that stills my heart and silences the enemy in Jesus' name. I have the mind of Christ, and I ask for revelation from heaven that shines light on God's truth."*

8. When you feel that the darkness is gone, ask God to fill you. Be at *peace* in His Presence where His love displaces all fear, confusion, and worry. Breathe it in.

9. Receive the Holy Spirit. "Lord, I open myself to Your Holy Spirit, to fill me and strengthen me and use me for Your purpose. I ask that You would fill me with Your light and Your love. Fill me with Your Holy Spirit in Jesus' name. I decree Your peace over my heart." Now breathe freedom in and let Him fill you completely.

10. Declare out loud, "I commit to living a righteous and holy life before You, Lord. I receive the freedom and power of Jesus over myself. I am free; I'm delivered, I'm healed! I decree it over myself. I am FREE in Jesus' mighty Name by the POWER of the blood of the Lamb; the same power that raised Jesus from the dead that is alive and well in me today; the same power that gives me LIFE to be victorious, LIFE to be holy, and power to make the right decisions. I am FREE in Jesus' name."

42

The Physical Healing Prayer

"Is any among you afflicted? let him pray. Is any merry? let him sing psalms. Is any sick among you? let him call for the elders of the church; and let them pray over him, <u>anointing him with oil</u> in the name of the Lord: And the prayer of faith shall save the sick, and the Lord shall raise him up; and if he have committed sins, they shall be forgiven him. Confess your faults one to another, and pray one for another, that ye may be healed. The effectual fervent prayer of a righteous man availeth much." (James 5:13-16)

Illnesses often vanish on their own after an individual has broken strongholds or encountered inner healing or deliverance. Notice in the following scripture how the physical healings come *after* the deliverances. *"When the even was come, they brought unto him many that were possessed with devils: and he cast out the spirits with his word, and healed all that were sick."* (Matthew 8:16) Do you believe in miracles? Matthew 19:26 tells us, *"With men this is impossible, but with God, all things are possible."* You need to begin expecting a miracle for physical healing when you anoint with oil. Pray the following prayer, trusting God completely:

"I pray for physical healing from stress and grief. I pray for total restoration in my body from all sickness and disease. Isaiah 53:5 says, 'with Your stripes I am healed.' I speak to my body, and I apply the blood of Jesus to you, now. I speak to every part of me, and I command you to line up with the Word of God that says you are healed and whole. I command you to function perfectly in Jesus' name. I speak peace, vitality, and resurrection life to every cell and I command you to come into alignment. I declare health and wholeness over my body. Be healed now, in Jesus' name, Amen."

43

The Stronghold Breaking Prayer

"Confess your faults one to another, and pray for one another that ye may be healed." (James 5:16)

The key to bringing down strongholds that have been constructed in our minds, is through strategic repentance. Breaking strongholds will strengthen the inner man and tear down the lies.

Fill out the *Negative Pattern Identification Form* in the back. Anoint with oil and pray the stronghold breaking prayers in the pages ahead by declaring each one aloud. Be sure to read chapter thirty-one on the steps to stronghold breaking as well.

"I repent of giving place to ____ (name the sin). Please forgive me, Lord. I am sorry for partnering with ____ (name the sin) instead of trusting You. I repent of all known and unknown generational sin. I ask for Your forgiveness to flow back through all generations of my family. I break every curse and vow that I have spoken or has been spoken over me. I break every agreement, covenant, sacrifice, and contract with ____ (name the

sin). I break every connection, every soul tie, and generational influence in my family lines with ____ (name the sin). I break all legal rights known and unknown. In the name of Jesus, I close all doors that I have opened to ____ (name the sin) in my life. I pull down every stronghold, and I take back all ground in the mighty name of Jesus. Thank You, Lord, for Your forgiveness and cleansing. I pray for a fresh outpouring of Your Holy Spirit over the places that ____ (name the sin) occupied. I ask You, Holy Spirit, to invade and possess this new territory. I invite You to rule and reign in this place. I ask that You bless me with boldness and confidence to trust You, in Jesus' name, Amen!"

Strongholds

44

ADDICTION

"What? know ye not that your body is the temple of the Holy Ghost which is in you, which ye have of God, and ye are not your own? For ye are bought with a price: therefore glorify God in your body, and in your spirit, which are God's." (1 Corinthians 6:19-20)

Keri was exhausted after her long days working at the hospital. The divorce had impacted her much more than she had wanted to admit and she found herself devastated by the loss of her marriage. She found herself much lonelier than she'd ever been.

Her brother had just been arrested for the second time with a DUI and was asking if he could stay with her again for a few weeks, which she knew meant until he could get another job. On top of it, Keri's ten-year-old, disabled daughter was scheduled for eye surgery.

When her daughter was a toddler, Keri found that a drink or two or three in the evening had calmed her down, especially because her husband was gone so much. After the divorce and the unexpected expenses, Keri had become an alcoholic.

She had been late to work for the fourth time this month, her car had broken down, and her boss had told her that if she missed another day of work that he would have to let her go. She didn't know how she was going to get to work or how she was going to be able to get her daughter to her doctor appointments.

Keri found herself drained mentally, emotionally, physically, and financially. Drinking had become her *way out* from feeling or expressing the emotion that had come with her grief. She felt her dreams slipping through her fingers. She began to drink a little more each month. She felt empty on the inside, and it scared her. Addiction had become the result of Keri's ungrieved losses.

Addiction always starts with harmless lies. *You need this. You deserve this. It's not a big deal. No one will know. You're an adult. You can make your own choices.* It's a lure of temptation usually brought in harmlessly and during a familiar stage of life.

It then can be used by the enemy during a rough season to hook a person. It can lead to terrible judgment, bad decision making, mistakes, and untimely death.

Temptation and addiction are shadowed by lies and deception. Addiction does not always pertain to drugs and alcohol. It can include areas such as food, gambling, sex, eating, and spending. The enemy's goal is to sabotage stability, success, and potential. Living in a constant state of grief for years and years can open the door to addiction, injustice, and prolonged grief.

Addiction does not add value to life; it subtracts value. The enemy uses addiction as a tool to destroy families, relationships, and careers. His plan is to devastate health and shatter dreams. He recognizes that a tormenting dependency can cause intelligent and creative people to compromise the things they value most. He knows that he can stop an amazing individual in their tracks, and he tries hard, especially when he sees their incredible potential.

The path addiction leads to is poverty, dysfunction, and trauma through abuse. Addiction can wreak havoc on a family, turning the dysfunction into a cycle that gets carried down by the children and passed on to future generations. It can destroy a person's identity when they lose the power to fight addiction over what they really value, time and time again. Once an addiction is full-blown, it can be almost impossible without God to break free.

You cannot have an addiction without hiding the truth to some degree. With addiction, you'll find deep deception, as they lie not only to others, but to themselves. Addicts learn to manipulate and their manipulation techniques such as denial become developed as a way of life. They usually hide behind these enhanced denial systems, minimizing their behaviors, and hurting those they love.

Addiction destroys trust when the addict takes what they want or need from others to support their habits. It can ruin relationships when the addict is dishonest and deceitful. Bluntly said, *addiction is sabotage.*

Addicts are often attracted to wholesome, flexible partners who want peace at any cost. These partners may have been raised by a parent who was an addict themselves and created a household of dysfunction; often they have learned to adapt well.

Living with an addict can be like living in a concentration camp. The partner must learn to set boundaries. These individuals often find themselves traumatized and suffering from PTSD after long term exposure to the lies. Two of the books cited earlier, *Safe People* by Henry Cloud and John Townsend and *In Sheep's Clothing* by Dr. George Simon are excellent resources for those who have been caught in the crossfire.

It's important to know that any involvement on the addict's part or the part of their ancestors in the area of the occult could have opened the door to the vulnerability of addiction. Did you know that when the stronghold is broken, that addiction will lose its magnetic power? If you've seen addiction plaguing and tormenting your friends or family or if you're an addict desperately hanging onto a thread of hope that you can be free, breaking this stronghold is imperative.

Additionally, most addicts will need Inner Healing, as they often suffer deeply from the wounds of profound loss. They may have compounded or consolidated losses that have not been grieved. Also, most addicts are impacted by intense guilt, which may have been generated initially by the death of a loved one.

<u>To break the power and stronghold of Addiction, use the steps in chapter thirty-one and speak this aloud:</u>

ADDICTION

"I confess all ..."

___Addictive Behaviors
___Deception
___Lies I've Told or Believed
___Confusion
___Frustration
___Pride
___Rebellion
___Witchcraft
___Religiosity
___Idolatry
___Guilt & Shame
___Compromise
___Betrayal of Myself & Others
___False Image of Myself or Others
___Denial
___Sexual Impurity
___Lust & Craving
___Poverty
___Wastefulness
___Wasted Time and Resources
___Rejection of Myself, Others or God
___Poor Choices
___Giving up or Giving in
___Selfishness
___Death & Destruction
___Destructive Habits

___Grief
___Emptiness, Sadness & Loneliness

"...and I confess it for myself, my parents, my grandparents, my great grandparents and all of my ancestors back to Adam... and I renounce its hold on my life and on my family line."

45

DOUBT & UNBELIEF

"But without faith it is impossible to please him: for he that cometh to God must believe that he is, and that he is a rewarder of them that diligently seek him." (Hebrews 11:6)

Doubt and unbelief are the greatest obstacles to our faith. Satan has been a deceiver from the beginning. In fact, the Bible tells us he is the "Father of Lies."

Satan uses darts to shoot ideas like fear, doubt, and unbelief at us. The sixth chapter of Ephesians tells us that we have been given spiritual armor and that we are to put it on. Part of our armor is the shield of *faith* which can quench the fiery darts of the devil. We are to use that shield when darts of doubt and unbelief are aimed at us.

"Now faith is the substance of things hoped for, the evidence of things not seen." (Hebrews 11:1) We must have *faith* in order to please God. Faith is the opposite of doubt and unbelief.

<u>To break the power and stronghold of Doubt & Unbelief, use the steps in chapter thirty-one and speak this aloud:</u>

DOUBT & UNBELIEF

"I confess ..."

____Doubt & Unbelief
____Questioning
____Suspicion
____Skepticism
____Lack of Trust
____Ungodly Opinion & Debate
____Choosing not to Believe
____Fear & Anxiety
____Worry
____Rejection
____Lack of Trust in God or in Others
____Double-Mindedness
____Involvement in the Occult
____Withdrawal
____Holding onto Disappointment

"...and I confess it for myself, my parents, my grandparents, my great grandparents and all of my ancestors back to Adam... and I renounce its hold on my life and on my family line."

46

FAILURE

"I can do all things through Christ which strengtheneth me." (Philippians 4:13)

People are hard-wired to need physical, tangible results from their work. Failure is strongly linked to limitation and being overwhelmed. The enemy wants to bring us to a place of perceived failure and impress hurt, grief, and bitterness upon us especially after a great loss.

Losses deserve to be acknowledged and grieved; otherwise we can get stuck and start to live in the past, becoming overwhelmed with guilt, regret, and remorse. Additionally, the enemy can then begin to bring in self-blame, shame, and condemnation which can move a person into a place of failure.

The enemy loves to shoot darts of failure at our mind, and the tricky part is that they usually take the *first-person* form. He wants us to think that the thoughts are ours. *I'm not smart. I'm weak. I'm not motivated. I don't have energy. I don't have talent. I don't have what it takes. I don't deserve what other people have.*

I'm not righteous enough. I can't afford to. It's impossible. I don't know how. I can't...

Often, the enemy will send darts labeled "fear of failure" which cause doubt of success and can hold an individual back from their dreams.

<u>To break the power and stronghold of Failure, use the steps in chapter thirty-one and speak this aloud:</u>

FAILURE

"I confess ..."

- ____ Failure
- ____ Infirmity
- ____ Lack of Accomplishment
- ____ Lack of Success
- ____ Lack of Direction
- ____ Lack of Roots
- ____ Sabotage
- ____ Miscarriage & Abortion
- ____ Bankruptcy
- ____ Deficiency & Deficit
- ____ Disappointment
- ____ Lost Hope, Lost Dreams, Lost Visions & Lost Goals
- ____ Lack of Motivation
- ____ Lack of Ambition
- ____ Limitation
- ____ Loss
- ____ Hopelessness
- ____ Perfectionism
- ____ Deterioration & Defeat

- ____ Poor Growth or Development
- ____ Bad Habits
- ____ Lack of Goal Setting
- ____ Lack of Follow Through or Consistency
- ____ Broken Promises
- ____ Procrastination
- ____ Distraction
- ____ Jumping from Project to Project
- ____ Lack of Focus
- ____ Insufficiency
- ____ Inability
- ____ Unconfessed Sin
- ____ Excuses
- ____ Giving Up
- ____ Passivity
- ____ Irresponsibility
- ____ Untrustworthiness
- ____ Lethargy & Laziness
- ____ Frustration
- ____ Wrong Beliefs
- ____ Being Accident Prone
- ____ Guilt
- ____ Neglect
- ____ Shame
- ____ Condemnation
- ____ Inadequacy
- ____ Fear of Success
- ____ Being Critical & all Criticism
- ____ Skepticism
- ____ Shooting down Ideas
- ____ Being Argumentative
- ____ Complaining & Pessimism
- ____ Lack of Contentment

____Heaviness
____Discouragement
____Misery
____Rejection
____Belief that Life is not going Well
____Negativity
____Fear of Things not being done Right
____Control
____Confusion
____Isolation
____Giving into being Overwhelmed
____Lack of Self- Worth
____Decisions to Give Up
____Sadness
____Grief
____Lack
____Wasted Time
____Wasted Potential

"...and I confess it for myself, my parents, my grandparents, my great grandparents and all of my ancestors back to Adam... and I renounce its hold on my life and on my family line."

47

FEAR

"Are not two sparrows sold for a farthing? and one of them shall not fall on the ground without your Father. But the very hairs of your head are all numbered. Fear ye not, therefore, ye are of more value than many sparrows." (Matthew 10:29-31)

Henry Wright discusses fear all throughout his book, *Be in Health*. It's worth the read if fear has been an area of torment for you. We must remember that fear is a spirit and that it's the direct opposite of God's love. *"God has not given us the spirit of fear, but power, love, and a sound mind."* (2 Timothy 1:7)

Many people do not realize that fear is one of the oldest tricks in the book. It works with a thieving spirit to steal opportunity, blessing, and hope and it works with a spirit of doubt to steal peace.

One of the enemy's tactics is to catastrophize situations and send darts with fearful scenarios of disaster striking. Has this ever happened to you? Here are some Biblical examples of fear: Fear kept Jonah from initially going to Nineveh. It caused King Saul to fear Goliath and the Philistines. Fear caused Elijah to crumble in the desert away from Jezebel. Fear caused Abraham to lie and say that his wife Sarah was his sister.

Wondering what you can do to stop fear in its tracks? Break the stronghold of fear and consider quoting the above scripture out loud whenever you feel fear. *"For God hath not given us the spirit of fear; but of power, and of love, and of a sound mind."* (2 Timothy 1:7)

In addition to breaking the stronghold of fear, allow the Lord to reveal specific events from the past that have opened the door to fear and go through inner healing for them. Additional support for this process can be found in the chapter on Fear in the *When the Heart Won't Let Go Workbook*.

A practical strategy you can take to remind yourself that you have overcome fear, is to write the fears you have previously dealt with on the bottom of your shoe (such as fear of abandonment, fear of failure, etc.) Each day it will be a reminder that it is under your feet and you will be making a statement to the enemy that you have authority over it.

<u>To break the power and stronghold of Fear, use the steps in chapter thirty-one and speak this aloud:</u>

FEAR

"I confess ..."

____Fears
____Phobias

____Torment in the Mind
____Anxiety
____Negativity
____Stress & Not dealing with Stress well
____Worry
____Being a People Pleaser
____Rejection & Fear of Rejection
____Bad Dreams & Night Terrors
____Occult Involvement
____Feelings of Dying or Suffocating
____Past Stories that have caused me Fear
____Books I've read or Movies I've watched that have caused me Fear
____Doubt & Unbelief
____Vows & Curses
____Lack of Trust in Myself, Others or God
____All the times I have not had Faith
____Giving in
____Ungodly Perfectionism
____Paranoia
____Giving in to being Overwhelmed
____Giving up Easily
____Withdrawing
____Dwelling on problems
____Not having Boundaries
____Procrastination
____Believing that my Opinion doesn't Matter
____Putting up Walls or being Guarded
____Control or Fear of being Controlled
____Fear of the Unknown
____Fear of Loss
____Fear of Failure
____Fear of Success

- ____ Fear of Disappointment
- ____ Fear of People
- ____ Fear of Death, Dying, or Loss
- ____ Fear of Accidents
- ____ Fear of Being Alone
- ____ Fear of Being Hurt
- ____ Fear of Being Vulnerable or Exposed
- ____ Fear of Intimacy
- ____ Fear of Being Loved
- ____ Fear to Love Completely
- ____ Fear of Past Experiences
- ____ Fear of Relationships
- ____ Fear of God
- ____ Fear of saying "No"
- ____ Fear of Speaking up or Speaking out
- ____ Fear of being Unsafe
- ____ Fear of being Unprotected
- ____ Fear of Rejection
- ____ Fear of Crowds & People
- ____ Fear of Trusting
- ____ Fear of Things not being done Right
- ____ Wasted Time
- ____ Wasted Potential

"...and I confess it for myself, my parents, my grandparents, my great grandparents and all of my ancestors back to Adam… and I renounce its hold on my life and on my family line."

After breaking the stronghold of fear, I encourage you to declare the following statement:

"I can do all things through Christ who strengtheneth me. I am free from all worry and anxiety. I am confident,

brave, and courageous. The Lord is my shepherd and He protects me. He watches over me and cares about everything that affects me. Even though I walk through the valley of the shadow of death, I will fear no evil for God is with me. God will never leave me or forsake me. His protection surrounds me like a shield. God gives me rest in peace as I live on this Earth. God's supernatural peace refreshes and restores my soul. God gives me sweet sleep. I refuse to be fearful or anxious about anything in my life. I cast all of my cares upon the Lord. God will not allow harm or evil to befall me. His strength and guidance take care of me in times of trouble. God's grace is sufficient for every area of my life. His Presence fills my soul. He is my refuge, my fortress, and my strong tower. I am not fearful concerning tomorrow. My future, my hopes, and my dreams are in God's hands. I know that God will fulfill His plans and purposes for me. He will deliver me from all of my enemies. I will lie down and sleep in peace, for He alone causes me to dwell in safety. The Lord is my strength and my shield. My heart trusts in Him, and I am helped."

48

IDOLATRY

"Love not the world, neither the things that are in the world. If any man love the world, the love of the Father is not in him. For all that is in the world, the lust of the flesh, and the lust of the eyes, and the pride of life, is not of the Father, but is of the world. And the world passeth away, and the lust thereof: but he that doeth the will of God abideth for ever." (1 John 2:15-17)

Idolatry is attributing a higher value to something than it should really have. It often takes the form of an object that contains great value to a person and can include a variety of material items and even people.

With idolatry, a person can be focused solely on themselves *or* they can hold things or people in extremely high esteem... higher than they should be held. When we idolize something or someone, we set the stage for disappointment.

Once I was helping a woman break strongholds. In our discussion, I felt led to ask how her relationship was with *food*. She told me that she thought about food a lot. She shared that while at work, she would daydream every afternoon about her dinner plans.

When she planned family vacations, instead of feeling excited for where she was headed and what she'd be doing, she'd continually evaluate the dinner menus. Plans for where and when she and her husband would eat and details of each course would consume her. She asked if that was normal and I told her that I didn't think so. We asked the Lord to show us what we were dealing with.

Immediately, we saw a picture of something that looked to be an altar and then realized it was an idol. On the front of it in large letters, was the word "FOOD." She acknowledged at that point that food had become an idol in her life.

We asked the Lord to reveal anything that could be connected to it and He showed us the words *deceit, desire, depression, and delusion.* The woman repented of giving in to any ungodly desire for food. She also repented of deceit, depression, delusion, and idolatry. We broke the stronghold of Idolatry and she became instantly set free. We also commanded all spirits of idolatry, deceit, desire, depression, and delusion to go in Jesus' name.

A few weeks later, she called me while on vacation in New York City. She told me that she and her husband had gotten really frustrated and that she had gone for a walk.

She passed by a bakery and heard the words, *"Get yourself a muffin. It will make you feel better."* She instantly recognized that the voice in her mind was not hers and realized that it was a lie. A muffin would not make her feel better. She recounted her surprise, when for the first time, she recognized that the voice she had always listened to was not *hers!*

She said out loud, *"No, a muffin will not make me feel better...working this out with my husband will make me feel better!"* and she turned around, walked back to the hotel, and worked things out with her husband. We knew she was truly free because she identified the conniving and convincing voice as being a dart from the enemy, instead of receiving it in as her own.

When thinking about idolatry, some idols that should be considered include: *Self, Family, an Individual, Money, Power, Materialism, Food, and Time.*

<u>To break the power and stronghold of Idolatry, use the steps in chapter thirty-one and speak this aloud:</u>

IDOLATRY

"I confess ..."

____Lack of True Identity
____Putting a person on a pedestal and believing they can do no wrong
____Areas in my Thought Life that get extreme amounts of Attention or Time
____Any Areas in my Life that are out of Balance
____Materialism
____Being Selfish
____Deception
____Fear & Anxiety
____Stubborness
____Fantasy

"...and I confess it for myself, my parents, my grandparents, my great grandparents and all of my ancestors back to Adam... and I renounce its hold on my life and on my family line."

49

IMAGE

"Thou shalt not bow down thyself unto them, nor serve them: for I the Lord thy God am a jealous God, visiting the iniquity of the fathers upon the children unto the third and fourth generation of them that hate me, And shewing mercy unto thousands of them that love me and keep my commandments." (Deuteronomy 5:9-10)

In the Bible, image is referred to many times as a *false image*. Imagine the golden calf that was designed and lifted up to worship while Moses was on the mountain with God. An image is a projection (like a portrait), and an image's purpose is to be lifted up to be worshiped.

The image that we have of ourself, is one we've constructed over the years that has been designed through things people have said to us and thoughts we've had about ourselves. Some people have an idea of how they want people to view them, and they will go to great lengths to protect their image and hold it up high. This thing that they are projecting is usually not their *true* self, and it causes them to live a lie. When pieces of their projected image start to fall apart, everything crumbles and the effects can be devastating.

Some people want to protect their past, so they are careful never to bring up certain truths. Some people are obsessed with themselves, but they don't want others to know. Instead of developing their character, some are very selfish, but go out of their way to appear selfless. Some try to hide certain aspects of themselves that they don't like. Some of these strategies might have been self-taught, and some may have been reflected onto one's identity in childhood. Sadly, all of these things lead to dishonesty with one's self and with others.

It takes a lot of effort and energy to maintain an image. The truth is, we want to be formed in the image of Christ. For that to happen, we must allow the Lord to break down the current image that we have of ourselves. To do that, we must break the stronghold of Image and allow the Lord to reveal our true identities to us and construct something in its place that glorifies Him.

<u>To break the power and stronghold of Image, use the steps in chapter thirty-one and speak this aloud:</u>

IMAGE

"I confess ..."

____Deception connected to my Image
____Stress & Anxiety
____False Image
____False Humility
____Lack of Confidence

____Not being able to truly accept a Compliment
____Idolatry
____Being Self-Absorbed
____Being Self Centered & Ungodly Focus on Myself and my Needs
____Inaccurate views of my Gifts, Skills, and Talents
____Self-Criticism
____Lack of True Identity
____Defensiveness
____Pride
____Fear of being Shamed or having a Poor Reputation
____Ungodly Focus on how Things will Look or how Things will appear to Others
____Offense
____Rejection
____Apologizing without Change
____Ungodly Focus on my Public Image or the Public Images of Others
____Being Defensive
____Needing Recognition
____Infirmity
____Extreme Focus on Problems in my Body
____Dissatisfaction with the Body that God gave Me

"...and I confess it for myself, my parents, my grandparents, my great grandparents and all of my ancestors back to Adam... and I renounce its hold on my life and on my family line."

50

IMPURITY

"I beseech you therefore, brethren, by the mercies of God, that ye present your bodies a living sacrifice, holy, acceptable unto God, which is your reasonable service. And be not conformed to this world: but be ye transformed by the renewing of your mind, that ye may prove what is that good, and acceptable, and perfect, will of God." (Romans 12:1-2)

Impurity refers to the perversion of purity. It is not surprising that the temptation of impurity comes very strongly to individuals who have a special call on their lives to represent the purity of God's character.

Impurity can include impure thoughts, impure dreams, lust, fornication, pornography, adultery, and all sexual deception and distortion. All of these symptoms are works of the flesh and encapsulate carnality.

Are we willing to set ourselves apart for the Lord, holy and pure? *"Wherefore come out from among them, and be ye separate, saith the Lord, and touch not the unclean thing; and I will receive you."* (2 Corinthians 6:17)

The Bible tells us to take every thought captive to the obedience of Christ Jesus. What this means is that when the darts of the devil are pointed at your mind and try to land, you reject them and disallow them from gaining any ground.

Imagine your mind as a landing strip. You intentionally want to protect your landing strip from enemy aircraft (the enemy's darts) so that they cannot land and gain entrance. The easiest way to do this is by using the shield of faith (a piece of our armor) to block the darts of the enemy.

To break the power and stronghold of Impurity, use the steps in chapter thirty-one and speak this aloud:

IMPURITY

"I confess all..."

____Lust
____Perversion
____Fornication
____Adultery
____Pornography
____Seduction
____Sexual Deception or Distortion
____Abuse
____Impure Thoughts
____Impure Dreams

"...and I confess it for myself, my parents, my grandparents, my great grandparents and all of my ancestors back to Adam... and I renounce its hold on my life and on my family line."

51

INDEPENDENCE & DIVORCE

"But I say unto you, That whosoever shall put away his wife, saving for the cause of fornication, causeth her to commit adultery: and whosoever shall marry her that is divorced committeth adultery." (Matthew 5:32)

I was sitting outside in the sun this morning reading Dr. Sumerall's Covenant workbook. In the second chapter, it says that a curse comes when a covenant is broken. I felt led to repent for all covenants that had been broken by my choices and by the decisions of the generations before me.

Even though I have never been divorced, I felt led to confess *sinning against God* and led to say *"I break any curse that came from breaking a covenant."* After I spoke the words, I closed my eyes and began to yawn. I literally began to *feel* a perception change. I started to think and feel a little differently. After about twenty minutes of soaking and sitting in the sun with my eyes closed yawning, I went into the house feeling very different.

Do you avoid conflict? Do you have a personal or family history of divorce? Do you tend to withdraw or lash out during arguments? Do you have a habit of abandoning relationships? Do people complain that they find it challenging to communicate with you?

If you answered yes to *any* of the above questions, it is highly recommended that you break the stronghold of Independence & Divorce.

<u>To break the power of Independence and Divorce, use the steps in chapter thirty-three and speak this aloud:</u>

INDEPENDENCE & DIVORCE

"I confess..."

____ Independence & Divorce
____ Insensitivity
____ Loneliness
____ Self-Determination
____ Playing the Devil's Advocate
____ Being Argumentative
____ Making Excuses
____ Being Withdrawn
____ Lack of Trust
____ Miscommunication
____ Involvement in the Occult
____ The Breaking of Covenant
____ Sinning against God

"...and I confess it for myself, my parents, my grandparents, my great grandparents and all of my ancestors back to Adam... and I renounce its hold on my life and on my family line."

52

LOSS & PROLONGED GRIEF

"And Jacob rent his clothes, and put sackcloth upon his loins, and mourned for his son many days." (Genesis 37:34)

Joanna, a seasoned teacher, opened the door to where she and her mother shared a home to find her mother lying in bed, white and cold. Shocked, her mind began to run scenarios. *What in the world had happened?* In desperation and dwindling hope, she dialed 911.

Her worst fears were confirmed as the medics pronounced her mother unresponsive from a heart attack. The next week was a complete blur as she wondered where God was and if He even cared.

Joanna's days bled into nights. She could hardly sleep between the nightmares, sobs, and waves of emotion. During the day she felt numb as she drove blindly through tears arranging her mother's service, flowers, and casket. Joanna's finances were tight and she found herself in a whirlwind, back at work just days later.

In the months that followed, she encountered a variety of challenges due to her foggy thinking, insomnia, and daydreaming. She found herself ladled with heavy guilt over her mother's death. She was confused and carried remorse and regret. She felt emotionally numb and started to withdraw socially. Deeply unmotivated, she slowly cleaned out her mother's room and the boxes in the garage. She was teary, overwhelmed, and depressed, feeling an empty hole in her heart that ached with sadness.

The feelings continued, draining her each week. Time seemed to drag out. She had somehow succumbed to a gloomy and emotionless cycle of Mondays and Fridays. She had given in to the lonely and quiet existence where her only friends were the sorrow and despair that accompanied her.

Eight years passed before a colleague encouraged Joanna to seek help for depression. It wasn't until she began to talk to a therapist that she recognized the prolonged grief. The therapist explained that dysfunctional grievers operate in a continual state of loss. Joanna learned that the stress of living in constant emotional pain was dangerous and could result in addiction and health problems.

She realized that prolonged grief had hijacked her life. The difference between grief and prolonged grief, her therapist explained, is that with prolonged grief, the typical stages are drawn out and begin to impact the person's life in a negative way. The individual becomes used to living with the pain, and the heart becomes continually heavy. It can be hard to understand why the process seems to last so long. Some recover quickly and some more slowly. Women tend to suffer from prolonged grief more often than men, and approximately one out of ten grievers move into prolonged grief.

Joanna agreed that she had carried the grief for too long and decided to do something about it. The next week she met with a prayer group that her therapist recommended. They helped her understand the process of inner healing and sent her home with resources. A few days later, while she was doing Listening Prayer and waiting on God, she saw a vision of the day her mother died. She saw her herself at the front door getting ready to unlock it. She was shocked to see Jesus standing next to her on the front porch. She watched almost like a movie, as she turned the key and walked in to see her mother. Jesus had walked in with her and was standing by her side. She couldn't bear to revisit the bedroom where she had first seen her mother, so instead, she turned to Jesus and He wrapped her in His arms. She buried her face in His chest and let the sobs come. For the first time since her mother had passed, she realized she wasn't alone. She saw the burden of grief on her shoulders like dark rain clouds and watched as Jesus took them and bore them as His own.

There is a fine line between allowing ourselves time and space to grieve and giving into prolonged grief or depression. Breaking strongholds and releasing soul ties has helped grievers who have suffered from every type of loss and painful event imaginable. It gets to the core of the grief, so the person can go on to lead a happy and healthy life.

Thankfully, God's Word contains this wonderful promise for us regarding grief. *"Thy sun shall no more go down; neither shall thy moon withdraw itself: for the LORD shall be thine everlasting light, and the days of thy mourning shall be ended."* (Isaiah 60:20)

Prolonged grief is often caused by a broken heart, a spirit of death, loss, grief, neglect, sadness, or guilt which can lead to deep darkness and depression. Loss, disappointment, and trauma are events that have the potential to become *traps of the enemy* by reigning us into a lifestyle of prolonged grieving. Trauma, loss, and death are events that deserve to be acknowledged and grieved; if they aren't, we can get stuck and start to live in the past.

There is a *significantly higher chance* of prolonged grief occurring in someone with an occult background or someone who has ancestors who participated in some level of occult involvement. I believe that prolonged grief can *appear* as a mood disorder, depression, bipolar disorder, and schizoaffective disorder. If prolonged grief is allowed to set in, it will assuredly progress to depression and can lead to a stronghold of Death.

To break the stronghold of Loss & Prolonged Grief, use the steps in chapter thirty-one and speak this aloud:

LOSS & PROLONGED GRIEF

"I confess ..."

____ Consistent Infirmity
____ Pressure
____ Loss
____ Withdrawal

- ____ Self-Absorption
- ____ Abuse of Myself or Others
- ____ Discouragement
- ____ Ignoring the Needs of Others
- ____ Relationship Difficulty
- ____ Escaping Reality
- ____ Isolation
- ____ Unrealistic Expectation of Myself or Others
- ____ Foggy Thinking
- ____ Negative Coping Strategies
- ____ Denial
- ____ Complaining
- ____ Negativity
- ____ Giving Up or Giving In
- ____ Indecision
- ____ Confusion
- ____ Insecurity
- ____ Disappointment
- ____ Shame
- ____ Rejection
- ____ Agitation
- ____ Heaviness of Heart
- ____ Lack of Progress
- ____ All Fear
- ____ Fear of Loss
- ____ Fear that Dreams or Desires will not come to Pass
- ____ Anxiety
- ____ Lost Hope
- ____ Lost Expectations of Things getting back to Normal
- ____ Guilt
- ____ Hopelessness
- ____ Discouragement

- ____ Depression
- ____ Exhaustion
- ____ Weariness
- ____ Fatigue
- ____ Loneliness
- ____ Sadness
- ____ Frustration
- ____ Powerlessness to Resist Opposition
- ____ Feelings of being Overwhelmed
- ____ Confusion
- ____ Failure & Feeling like a Failure
- ____ Regret
- ____ Hurt
- ____ Pain
- ____ Deep Loss
- ____ Injustice
- ____ Moodiness
- ____ Negative Talk
- ____ Anger
- ____ Angry Outbursts
- ____ Impulsive or uncharacteristic Decision Making
- ____ Anxiety or Panic Attacks
- ____ Loss of Motivation
- ____ Loss of Inner Joy

"...and I confess it for myself, my parents, my grandparents, my great grandparents and all of my ancestors back to Adam... and I renounce its hold on my life and on my family line."

53

NEGATIVITY

"In everything give thanks: for this is the will of God in Christ Jesus concerning you." (1 Thessalonians 5:18)

An individual with a negative outlook would do well to look inside and ask themselves what's going on in their heart. *Where are they hurting?*

Negative individuals do not make enjoyable company. Their pessimistic and complaining spirit causes them to be shunned and avoided, thus further deepening their feelings and rejection. Negativity always points to a deeper root.

Often a person with a negative outlook is holding onto an injustice or is bitter about something. They might be grieving or may have experienced a deep, personal trauma that has made them skeptical. It will be good for this individual to do some soul searching.

The answer could lie in something as simple as rejection. Rejection happens in the heart and is usually covered up by walls. Did you know that gratefulness opposes negativity? A negative individual can train themselves to be more positive by focusing on the things in which they are grateful.

<u>To break the power and stronghold of Negativity, use the steps in chapter thirty-one and speak this aloud:</u>

NEGATIVITY

"I confess all..."

____Negativity
____Judgment
____Accusation
____Criticism
____Blame
____Control
____Doubt & Unbelief
____Frustration
____Irritation
____Complaining
____Strife & Contention
____Impatience
____Bad Attitudes
____Negative words
____Profane Words or Thoughts
____Word Curses I've spoken over Myself or Others

"...and I confess it for myself, my parents, my grandparents, my great grandparents and all of my ancestors back to Adam... and I renounce its hold on my life and on my family line."

54

RELIGIOSITY

"Quench not the Spirit." (1 Thessalonians 5:19)

Bob Jones, a powerful seer, and prophet to our generation once said, *"Waiting upon the Lord essentially has been a lost art in the corporate Church. It is imperative that we begin to understand this great spiritual principle in accomplishing the divine purposes established for this generation."* Bob often shared a revelation he received on the story of Mary and Martha that taught him to wait at the feet of the Father to receive instruction. Even as Mary sat at the Lord's feet admiringly embracing truth, *so also did the Lord sit at the Father's feet receiving His counsel.*[5]

Bob taught that if we can faithfully follow the example of Mary in this season of the Spirit, we will also receive counsel from the Lord to accomplish the will of the Father. He believed that the Lord desires to change our mindset from that of Martha to Mary, so that we no longer labor for Him and begin to work *with* Him.

Often those following the example of Martha will seemingly persecute those sitting at the Lord's feet waiting on Him. It can be challenging to overcome the tendency to continually be busy about "religious activity." There is definitely something profound to be said for waiting at the feet of the Lord for direction.

Some symptoms of a religious spirit can include control, accusation, judgment, pride, confrontation, quenching of the Holy Spirit, strife, contention, lack of agape love, rejection, legalism, fear, bossy opinions, oppression of others, slander, division, doubt, unbelief, and micromanaging.

The following "Fifteen Signs of a Religious Spirit" is derived from the book of Jude and from Jack Deere's teaching *Exposing the Religious Spirit*.[6] This list delineates a spectrum of expressions of the religious mindset. Manifestations of the religious spirit are not limited to Christianity and can be identified in any false religion as well.

1. Rift: One with a religious spirit believes he has a mission to tear down error or what he believes is wrong.

2. Rebuke: He has a hard time receiving a rebuke from someone less spiritual than he.

3. Rebellious: He will not listen to people, because he can hear from God.

4. Repulsed: He immediately notices what is *wrong* with people, or the church, rather than what is *right*.

5. Rigorous: He keeps score on his spiritual life and carries guilt when he doesn't add up to the Lord's standards.

*6. Rejecting***:** He feels as though he has been appointed to fix everybody else.

7. Rival: He may feel as though he is truly closer to God than others, and that his life or ministry is more pleasing to God in comparison.

8. Ranks: He takes pride in spiritual discipline or spiritual maturity and ranks himself against others.

9. Reputation: He will do things to be noticed or affirmed by people.

10. Rigid: Religious spirits are overly repulsed by "emotionalism."

11. Raucous: Seemingly converse to the prior, a religious spirit will use emotionalism or hype to manipulate people.

12. Resistant: He will tend to resist the supernatural or reject spiritual manifestations he cannot understand.

13. Reactionary: He will overreact to carnality or immaturity in the body of Christ.

14. Renegade: He will not fully commit to a church or lend a hand to help if the group is not *perfect* in their theology.

15. Refrain: He will tend to be suspicious of or even oppose new moves of God.

---

[5] Jones, B., *You are My Friend* (Great Faith Publishing, 2010).
[6] https://definingwords.wordpress.com/2012/04/27/15-signs-of-a-religious-spirit/

<u>To break the power and stronghold of Religiosity, use the steps in chapter thirty-one and speak this aloud:</u>

RELIGIOSITY

"I confess ..."

____Control
____Manipulation
____Judgment
____Spiritual Pride
____Denial
____Bitterness & Unforgiveness
____Resentment
____Holding onto Injustice
____Confrontation
____Strife & Contention
____Ungodly Opinion or Debate
____Quenching of the Holy Spirit
____Lack of Agape love
____Lack of Self-Assessment
____Times I have not loved my Neighbor as Myself
____Lack of Deep, Committed Relationships
____Carrying Wounds
____Legalism
____Anger
____Profanity
____All Racism & Prejudice
____Frustration & Confusion
____Impatience & Insensitivity
____Doubt & Unbelief
____Rejection
____Fear & Anxiety
____Oppression of Others

____Intimidation or Abuse
____Micromanaging
____Dealing Poorly with Stress
____Possible Wrong Doctrine or Misuse of Scripture
____Ungodly Perfection
____Rigid Moral Codes
____Failure
____Negativity
____Criticism
____Condemnation
____Accusation
____Discouragement
____Idolatry
____Materialism
____Rebellion
____Lack of a Desire to Change
____Allowing my Prophetic Gift to be Perverted
____Desiring Recognition or seeking Position
____Guilt in trying to overcome Fleshly or Worldly Desires
____Instability
____Lack of Self-Control or Self-Discipline
____Being Unaccountable
____Self-Righteousness
____Seeking Religious busyness or Activity
____Lack of true Identity in Christ
____All False Identity based on Works
____Being Hypocritical & all Hypocrisy
____Having a Martyr Complex
____Making Excuses
____All Spiritual Deception & Fantasy
____Any Lies I've Told or Believed
____Secrets

____Guilt, Shame & Regret
____Fear of being Shamed or having a poor Reputation
____Ungodly Focus on how Things will Look or how Things will appear to Others
____Offense
____Condescending Attitudes & Behaviors
____Division & Conflict

"..and I confess it for myself, my parents, my grandparents, my great grandparents and all of my ancestors back to Adam… and I renounce its hold on my life and on my family line."

READ AN EXCERPT FROM

BOOK 3 IN THE
BREAKING NEGATIVE PATTERNS
SERIES

Coming Next

Cleansing your Property: Establishing a Perimeter of Holiness In and Around Your Home

A few years ago, my husband and I got a call from a friend who we've known for over two decades. He lived alone and had been experiencing some strange things in his home. In the middle of the night, while he was sleeping, his bed had been shaken and banged up against the wall. He had never experienced anything like it before and was calling for some advice and spiritual support. We identified that this was a spiritual problem and knew it would be simple to resolve. It was apparent immediately that the enemy was harassing him through fear and intimidation.

We knew because he believed in Christ, that the enemy had no right to harass him in his own home or on his property. The only legal right that the enemy could've had was if our friend had failed to initially cleanse the property when he moved in or if he had brought in an object with something demonic attached to it or allowed something (or someone) evil in his home. We asked him about this, and he explained that he had never spiritually cleansed the property when he originally moved in years before. Because of this, there was a door left open for the enemy to harass him.

Did you know that you can stand in the gap and repent for the sins that have occurred on your property before you took ownership? We have done this many times. You are spiritually cleansing the property, as well as neutralizing it, which releases the enemy's legal right to harass or cause problems on the site now or in the future. Once that is done, you can release heavenly things onto the property such as love, peace, joy, and even angelic protection. Covering prayer secures the perimeter and protects it from demonic infiltration. There is an instant shift that happens in the spirit that can be felt. When the peace of God comes and flows over your property, there is nothing like it in the world. Even visitors will comment on how peaceful it feels.

We agreed to meet with our friend the very next day at his home so we could spiritually cleanse his home and property, and also teach him how to help others to do the same. One of the things we've learned in ministry is that every ministry opportunity is a training opportunity. Once you experience a breakthrough in an area, it is highly likely that God will lead you to help others through similar discoveries.

Did you know that you retain approximately 90% of what you attempt to teach others? As you're learning new techniques, and sharing strategies with those around you, you're cementing each new concept that you learn. Think of all the people who you can help after you cleanse your property!

We always encourage people when they buy a new home or piece of land, or sign a new lease, that along with their signature on the line and transference to their name, that they spiritually cleanse the property. If you are a property owner of multiple units, we recommend the covering prayer for your properties at the end of each lease.

It is impossible to know what iniquity was committed on a piece of land in time past. We do know that life is in the blood and that blood has a voice and can call out from the ground. Leviticus 17:11 confirms *"For the life of the flesh is in the blood"* and in Genesis 4:10, we read that Abel's blood cried out from the ground after he was murdered; *"And he said, What hast thou done? the voice of thy brother's blood crieth unto me from the ground."*

Covering Prayer for a Home and Property

When we arrived at our friend's house, the first thing we did was establish a perimeter of holiness around his property. We started at the front corner. Using oil to represent the blood of Jesus, we walked in a group as close to the perimeter as possible, anointing the fence every ten to twenty feet. We prayed through each corner of the property, repenting for sin that had been committed in the past, and covered each side with the blood of Jesus until we came back to the starting point.

We prayed a prayer like this. *"Lord, as we take this oil, that represents the blood of Jesus, we apply it to every inch of the perimeter of this property. We cover every part of this property with the blood of Jesus. We confess all sin that has been committed here, and we repent for all bloodshed that has taken place on this land. We ask You, Lord, that You would begin to purify and cleanse this land with your blood. We pray God that you would release a river of living water from heaven to spiritually neutralize and cleanse this property from front to back and from top to bottom. We ask You for a spiritual shield as a cover of protection; we ask for a foundation of protection below the entire property and all the buildings on the property.*

We ask that You would release your Presence here on this land and that Your glory would flow over it. Lord, we ask that You would lift a banner of peace over this property and that You would wave a banner of love and joy over this land. We ask You God to position angels on the four corners of this property, to stand guard in Jesus' name, Amen."

Next, we spoke to all demonic entities that had been around. *"In Jesus' name, we take authority over every foul thing that has lingered here, that has had a right to be here in the past, and that has continued to operate and harass our friend. We bind you now in the name of Jesus. We command you to go. You loose your hold over this property and this land right now in Jesus' name."* We knew that these prayers would instantly remove demonic access.

We then walked into the house together. We gave our friend instructions, that as a team we would be anointing every door, every threshold, every window and mirror, and any other places or things that the Lord would point out. We asked the Holy Spirit to highlight anything in the home that was unholy.

In his bedroom, we went to the head of the bed, and anointed the headboard and wall with oil. We said, *"In Jesus' name we take authority over the spirit of fear, and we bind you right now. You take your hands off of this bed. You loose your hold right now in the name of Jesus. The blood of Jesus Christ is against you. Now you go off this property up to the throne of God to be dealt with by Him."* I like to send them to God's throne, but where they are commanded to go is up for debate.

I've heard of them being sent to "the pit." In studying where Jesus sent them, we see a variety of places, including swine.

Each of us took anointing oil and spread out into different parts of the house, working as a team, anointing and praying. The prayers were almost identical to the prayers we had prayed for the land. *"We ask You, Lord, to cover this home with the blood of Jesus. We ask You to pour Your blood over every wall, over the ceiling and the foundation of this home. We repent for all sin that has been committed on this property. We command every unclean spirit to leave. We ask You, Lord, to send a mighty wind to blow them out and to pour out Your Presence here. We ask that this home be full of the atmosphere of heaven and that You release angels to stand guard at the doors. We dedicate this home and property to You to be used for Your glory. We seal these prayers with the blood of Jesus. We bless this home and we bless this property in Jesus' name."*

There are no perfect words to use. Be led by the Spirit. You are welcome to use these prayers as examples; however, you cannot go wrong as long as you are using the name of Jesus and showing the enemy that you are walking in your authority. You walk in your authority by putting your shoulders back, speaking in a strong voice to the enemy, walking in faith, and believing in your position as a child of God. You will have no problem closing the spiritual doors and taking back your legal rights when you remind yourself of the promises that God has given you. For example, Isaiah 32:18 says, *"And my people shall dwell in a peaceable habitation, and in sure dwellings, and in quiet resting places."*

In Psalm 27:1, David states, *"The LORD is my light and my salvation; whom shall I fear? the LORD is the strength of my life; of whom shall I be afraid?"* Proverbs 18:10 tells us that *"The name of the LORD is a strong tower: the righteous runneth into it, and is safe."*

All of these promises can be quoted and stood upon. Remember, God's word cannot return void to Him. Cleansing your home may feel uncomfortable at first, but after practicing, this will become second nature to you. Psalms 91 is the perfect passage of scripture to read aloud as you start a spiritual cleanse for a property or business. We know that when Jesus was pushing back the enemy in His personal life, He quoted scripture directly to him. As you declare Psalm 91, you are establishing a scriptural foundation of protection.

"He that dwelleth in the secret place of the most High shall abide under the shadow of the Almighty. I will say of the Lord, He is my refuge and my fortress: my God; in him will I trust. Surely he shall deliver thee from the snare of the fowler, and from the noisome pestilence. He shall cover thee with his feathers, and under his wings shalt thou trust: his truth shall be thy shield and buckler. Thou shalt not be afraid for the terror by night; nor for the arrow that flieth by day; Nor for the pestilence that walketh in darkness; nor for the destruction that wasteth at noonday. A thousand shall fall at thy side, and ten thousand at thy right hand; but it shall not come nigh thee. Only with thine eyes shalt thou behold and see the reward of the wicked. Because thou hast made the Lord, which is my refuge, even the most High, thy habitation; There shall no evil befall thee, neither shall any plague come nigh thy dwelling. For he shall give

his angels charge over thee, to keep thee in all thy ways. They shall bear thee up in their hands, lest thou dash thy foot against a stone. Thou shalt tread upon the lion and adder: the young lion and the dragon shalt thou trample under feet. Because he hath set his love upon me, therefore will I deliver him: I will set him on high, because he hath known my name. He shall call upon me, and I will answer him: I will be with him in trouble; I will deliver him, and honour him. With long life will I satisfy him, and shew him my salvation."

Back to our friend... after we prayed with him at his property, there were no more problems with his bed moving at night. He didn't have any more interferences in his sleep or anxiety in his home. There had been a spiritual line drawn. The enemy wasn't welcome anymore.

NEGATIVE PATTERN IDENTIFICATION FORM

Score yourself based on a scale where 5 is extremely frequent and 0 is never. Numbers between 0-5 represent the frequency.

ADDICTION
___ Addictive Behaviors
___ Guilt & Shame
___ Rejection
___ Destructive Habits

ANGER
___ Angry Thoughts
___ Underlying Anger
___ Holding onto Injustice
___ Violence

BITTERNESS
___ Carrying Wounds
___ Retaliation
___ Resentment
___ Unforgiveness

CONFUSION
___ Distraction
___ Indecisiveness
___ Frustration
___ Lack of Direction

CONTROL
___ Lack of Trust
___ Control
___ History of Trauma
___ Manipulation

DEATH
___ Grief
___ Gloom
___ Oppression
___ Depression
___ Destruction

DECEPTION
___ Excuses
___ Daydreams and Lost time
___ Illusions
___ Rationalizations

DISCOURAGEMENT & DEPRESSION
___ Oppression
___ Hopelessness
___ Discouragement
___ Despair

DOUBT & UNBELIEF
___ Questioning
___ Suspicion
___ Skepticism
___ Ungodly Opinion & Debate

DYSFUNCTION
___ Abuse
___ Lack of Boundaries
___ Dysfunctional Relationships
___ Demands, Pressure & Expectations

FAILURE
___ Infirmity
___ Lack of Accomplishment
___ Lack of Success
___ Sabotage

FATIGUE
___ Giving Up or Giving In
___ Heaviness /Consistent Exhaustion
___ Powerlessness to Resist Opposition
___ Delays

FEAR
- ___ Fears
- ___ Phobias
- ___ Worry
- ___ Anxiety

FREEMASONRY
- ___ Problems with any of the five Senses including the Eyes, Ears, Nose, Taste or Touch
- ___ History of Financial Frustration
- ___ Accidents
- ___ Injuries
- ___ Discord in Family

GUILT & SHAME
- ___ Guilt & Shame
- ___ Hurt & Pain
- ___ Blame
- ___ Rejection of Self, God or Others

HOPE DEFERRED
- ___ Sadness
- ___ Disappointment
- ___ Hopelessness
- ___ Discouragement

HUMILIATION
- ___ Distractions & Inability to Focus
- ___ Being Unresponsive
- ___ Neglect & Rejection of Self or Others
- ___ Pressure

IDENTITY
- ___ Changing Behavior based on who I'm around
- ___ Feeling of Hiding Behind a Mask
- ___ Being Unsure of Self, Direction, or Beliefs
- ___ Lack of Confidence

IDOLATRY
- ___ Areas in Thought Life that get extreme Amounts of Attention and Time
- ___ An Area of Life that is out of Balance
- ___ Materialism

*Idols can include: Self, Family, Money, and Food

IMAGE
- ___ Fear of being Shamed or Having a Poor Reputation
- ___ Ungodly Focus on how Things will Look or how Things will Appear to Others
- ___ Offense
- ___ Self-Focused

IMPURITY
- ___ Impure Thoughts
- ___ Impure Dreams
- ___ Abuse
- ___ Perversion

INDEPENDENCE & DIVORCE
- ___ Independence & Divorce
- ___ Self-Determination
- ___ Being Argumentative
- ___ Miscommunication

INFIRMITY
- ___ Sickness
- ___ Disease
- ___ Chronic Physical Problems
- ___ Exhaustion with Debilitating Pain

INJUSTICE
- ___ Defiance and Non-compliance
- ___ Resentment at the Thought of Being Controlled
- ___ Holding onto Injustice
- ___ Lack of Cooperation

JEZEBEL
- ____ Abusive Behaviors, Abusive Attitudes & Holding onto Abuse
- ____ Betrayal, Treachery & Lack of Faithfulness
- ____ Lack of Genuine Love or Affection
- ____ Lack of Accountability

NEGATIVITY
- ____ Criticism
- ____ Complaining
- ____ Negative Words or Attitudes
- ____ Blame

NEW AGE/ANTICHRIST
- ____ Mental Illness
- ____ Mental Torment or Bi-Polar Tendencies
- ____ Psychic Experiences
- ____ Confusion

PERFECTION
- ____ Perfectionism
- ____ Being Critical & all Criticism
- ____ Lack of Contentment
- ____ Fear of Things not being Done Right
- ____ Control

POVERTY/GREED
- ____ Losing or Breaking things of Worth
- ____ Poor Financial Choices
- ____ Emotional Spending
- ____ Hard Work with Nothing to Show

PRIDE
- ____ Pride
- ____ Racism / Prejudice
- ____ Condescending Attitudes
- ____ Judgment

REBELLION
- ____ Being Resistant / Self-Willed
- ____ Stubbornness
- ____ Insubordination
- ____ Disobedience

REJECTION
- ____ Disappointment
- ____ Feeling Unloved or Unworthy
- ____ Inferiority / Inadequacy
- ____ Rejecting Myself, Others, or God

RELIGION
- ____ Confrontation
- ____ All False Identity based on Works
- ____ Seeking Religious Busyness or Activity
- ____ Guilt in Overcoming Fleshly or Worldly Desires
- ____ Strong Will to Voice Opinion or Debate

SPIRITISM/WITCHCRAFT
- ____ Being Sharp with the Tongue
- ____ Divorce / Division / Contention
- ____ Dark Fears
- ____ Any Involvement in the Occult

STRESS & ANXIETY
- ____ Pressure
- ____ Stress & Anxiety
- ____ Fears
- ____ Physical Symptoms connected to Stress

TIME MANAGEMENT
- ____ Procrastination
- ____ Stress & Anxiety around Appointments
- ____ Resentment around Agreeing to Obligations
- ____ Fear of Commitment or Obligation

Miscellaneous Information

*To find downloadable copies of all of the strongholds, go to www.goldlanternmedia.com

*Find us on Facebook under the public group Breaking Negative Patterns.

*The mystery box that arrived on Allie's doorstep contained a supplement called *Raw Thyroid* by Natural Sources.

*The anointing oil we use is *Frankincense* essential oil. After researching, Eli and I have found essential oils which we believe are of utmost purity and highest quality. If you don't have someone you know to get high quality essential oils through, it would be a blessing, and we would be honored for you to order through our member number. To order an essential oils kit, call 1 (800) 371-3515 and mention enroller and sponsor number 2811388 or go to www.youngliving.com and use the number there. Most people begin with the *Premium Starter Kit* which comes with eleven oils (including frankincense, lavender, lemon, and peppermint) and a diffuser to release the vapors and health benefits into your home or work space.

COMING NEXT
IN THE
BREAKING NEGATIVE PATTERNS
SERIES

Book 3
Includes the strongholds of *Anger, Hope Deferred, Humiliation, Infirmity, Poverty, Pride, Rebellion, Stress, Anxiety,* and *Time Management.*

Book 4
Includes the strongholds of *Death, Freemasonry, Guilt, Shame, Identity, Jezebel, Negativity, New Age / Anti-Christ, Perfection, Rejection* and *Spiritism/Witchcraft (occult).*

About the Author

Lisa Tyson was born in Oxnard, California. The first two years of her life were filled with trips to Children's Hospital in Los Angeles where she underwent six surgeries to reconstruct genetic internal defects. She healed well and became very active, loving her roller skates and enjoying sports. Lisa became determined to live life to its fullest.

Lisa's father is a pastor who was born in Great Britain and raised in South Africa. From an early age, she was told stories about faraway places and often visited England. During high school, Lisa volunteered in emergency, pediatrics and the neonatal unit at the local hospital, developing a keen empathy and compassion for those who were in pain and were alone.

Lisa has a passion for helping people find freedom. She loves missions and traveling to other nations. She has visited dozens of countries and has traveled to every state in the U.S. Her heart is to protect the vulnerable and support the hurting. Lisa's days are filled with writing and stronghold breaking ministry. In the future, Lisa and her husband, Eli see themselves running an orphanage in Brazil.